PETERSEN'S

HUNTING
Guide to
WHITETAIL
DEER

PETERSEN'S

HUNTING
Guide to
WHITETAIL
DEER

A COMPREHENSIVE GUIDE TO HUNTING OUR COUNTRY'S FAVORITE BIG-GAME ANIMAL

PETERSEN'S HUNTING
INTRODUCTION BY MIKE SCHOBY

Skyhorse Publishing

Skyhorse Publishing books may be purchased in bulk at special discounts for sales promotion, corporate gifts, fund-raising, or educational purposes. Special editions can also be created to specifications. For details, contact the Special Sales Department, Skyhorse Publishing, 307 West 36th Street, 11th Floor, New York, NY 10018 or info@ skyhorsepublishing.com.

Skyhorse® and Skyhorse Publishing® are registered trademarks of Skyhorse Publishing, Inc.®, a Delaware corporation.

Visit our website at www.skyhorsepublishing.com.

10 9 8 7 6 5 4 3 2

Library of Congress Cataloging-in-Publication Data is available on file.

Cover design by Tom Lau
Cover photo credit: Dale C. Spartas

Print ISBN: 978-1-5107-1312-3
Ebook ISBN: 978-1-5107-1318-5

Printed in the United States of America

TABLE OF CONTENTS

INTRODUCTION

By Mike Schoby, Editor, *Petersen's Hunting* Magazine

It has been twenty-five years since I shot my first whitetail and I am still amazed by *Odocoileus virginianus*. Think about it—what other big game species inhabits such varied terrain, across a massively broad range, are so intelligent and adaptable, and provided millions of hunters an incredible hunting opportunity, not to mention a wonderful food source?

As I wrote this, I paused to look out of my window at the distant snow-capped Bitterroot Mountains that hem in my Western Montana home. Several hundred yards from my window, a pair of whitetail does saunter through an aspen grove surrounded by sage flats—not what most would think of as "typical" whitetail habitat, but there they are, thriving in a place more commonly associated with elk and mule deer.

And that is really what makes the whitetail so special—they thrive nearly coast to coast. Over the years, I have hunted them from Washington all the way to New Brunswick and from the Mexican border in Texas to our northern border in Wisconsin. And that is just in the continental United States—no other species transcends borders like the whitetail. Incredible hunting can be had in Canada and Mexico with subspecies stretching all the way to South America.

If that isn't enough range for you, consider the fact that North American whitetails have been transplanted around the world to places like New Zealand and Norway where they thrive—spawning a whitetail culture of rattling, scents, and treestands to countries not previously accustomed to such.

A hunter could spend a lifetime hunting whitetails in a different state/province/country every year and not see it all. That is truly impressive, but what is even more impressive is no matter where you live, you really don't ever have to travel far to hunt America's most popular deer. That is the real key to their charm—they are everyman-accessible; from a patch of state ground in Pennsylvania to the family farm in Iowa.

Sure, a chance at a huge buck increases on well-managed (and often high dollar) private land, but it is not always the case. Peruse the record books, and do some research on the top twenty entries and see how many of those bucks came from guided or high dollar hunts—very few. The story is almost always the same, magnificent bucks are killed every year by an average Joe, who got off work a couple hours early, ran to his stand, and lo and behold a world-class deer strolled by.

I like to think about that every time I hunt whitetails. While my odds of ever winning the lottery are slim to none, I know that no matter where I am hunting there is always a chance of a record-class buck trotting by in pursuit of a hot doe. Even if no wall-hanger appears, there is always an excellent chance a doe will appear to fill my freezer and that is reason enough to pursue this magnificent animal.

SECTION ONE
FEATURES

MIDWEST WHITETAILS

A tough season, but a

GOOD ONE.

CRAIG BODDINGTON

Five days before the Kansas rifle season, I sat in my stand with my mom and aunt. During the spring and summer, I'd burned and, with a lot of help, cleared, leveled and planted. Thanks to perfect rains, my winter wheat had come up nicely, and the deer loved it. Now, on the eve of the season, I was hoping to show the ladies some of our Kansas whitetails. Of course, I was also doing some last-minute scouting.

That was the slowest of any evening I sat that stand, but two of the six does that came in fed right in front of us. We had a great evening, not too cold, and just when it was getting dim, I saw one more deer step out of the woods. It was so dark I was the only one to see him, but through good glass I saw him very clearly. He was tall, wide and heavy, his only flaw being he was missing his G-4 on one side, making him a nine-pointer. He came in like he owned the place, and I was pretty sure that when the season opened I'd own him if I wanted to.

Two days later—three days before rifle season—I borrowed my neighbor's Kawasaki mule, and at noon on a sunny day we took a little family excursion around the farm. We roused several does from their beds, and then, along a tree line, I caught the flash of an antler.

At their Kansas place, the author and his family don't take their scouting seriously, but it was during this family game drive that the biggest buck was seen. The author is flanked, left to right, by his dad's sister, Betty Reese; his mom, Jeanne Boddington; and his daughter, Brittany.
Photo Credit: Craig Boddington

The author's primary food plot is winter wheat, and the deer seemed to love it. From late October through the rifle season, the deer hit it hard every evening. However, after rifle season started, the bucks were moving only at night.
Photo Credit: Craig Boddington

Oh, Lord, this was a buck. He was a dream Kansas whitetail, a perfect 10-pointer, heavy and tall. He was the buck I wanted to find when rifle season opened.

FIRST SEASON
Do you want suspense, or do you want honesty? Forget the former; deal with the latter: I never saw either buck again. Anybody would have shot that 10-pointer—and everybody in the neighborhood would have known. So I'm pretty sure he went to ground. The other buck, well, both my wife, Donna, and my buddy Jim Jurad, who joined us for the first part of the season, saw pretty good bucks in poor light, but either they weren't sure enough to shoot or they chose to hold out. If they saw that nine-pointer, their decisions were poor.

A couple of years ago, with somewhat imperfect knowledge of what the economy was going to do, Donna and I bought a little farm in southeast Kansas. I'm from Kansas originally, but not from this part of the state, and in fact I'd never even set foot in the county where, almost sight unseen, I was suddenly a landowner. I'm sure it was temporary insanity.

The area is beautiful, a southern extension of the Flint Hills, with

Oklahoma's sand hills are unusual habitat, scenic in their way and very good whitetail habitat. There's a good buck out there, and Joey Meibergen is trying to find him, but the buck vanished into one of the countless little draws.

Photo Credit: Craig Boddington

Kansas allows the use of feeders, so the author put in a good one to help concentrate the does. The chances of taking a mature buck on the corn are pretty slim, but the more does you can have feeding in daylight, the better.
Photo Credit: Craig Boddington

The author put one tower stand overlooking a primary food plot, a well-made hexagonal design from HB Hunting Products. It's a lot easier to sit when you can move around a bit. When it got really cold, ladder stands and tree stands were out of the question.
Photo Credit: Craig Boddington

thick oak ridges. Pretty much on a whim, we had told my buddy Kirk Kelso and his wife, Roxane, to keep their eyes out for a nice piece of ground. Next thing I knew, I was figuring out how to drive a tractor, only hurting myself once or twice. I was also trying to learn the right food crops to plant and how to keep Donna from discovering how much a good deer stand actually costs. I think we planted the right stuff, because through the season our daily average on the food plot was 18 whitetails. As for the other, well, I wasn't there when the manufacturer delivered our primary stand, so I got busted big-time. At least, as Donna had insisted, it was insulated and windproof—pretty comfy, too.

We could have hunted our place in the 2008 season, but I had this little matter of a desert sheep tag to deal with. None of it had been farmed for a decade and more, so I was glad for the extra year to set up things. We burned and cleared and planted, and I took on board a lot of advice. Some was from bowhunt-er Shane Johnson, son of the folks we bought the place from. He had permission to hunt, so he sited a couple of ladder stands in the woods, our agreement being that he'd leave them in place for the rifle season. I had a tripod stand as well, and I moved it three times during the season.

NOVEMBER

People from eastern states such as Illinois (and northern states such as Minnesota) define things differently, but in my lexicon, Kansas and its immediate neighbors constitute the Midwest. Our deer rut in November. The Kansas rifle season is early December, set up many years ago to be a post-rut season. Although this is very bad for rifle hunters, it is very good for bowhunters, who have a November season. If you want to hunt the Kansas rut, take a bow or go north to Nebraska or south to Oklahoma where rifle seasons coincide with the rut.

I haven't had my bow out of mothballs for years, so I confined my Kansas rut hunting to scouting—and keeping my ears open. I didn't get much help from Shane. He sat one of his stands one morning, and after an exhausting 15-minute wait, he arrowed a nice buck. Kirk was more helpful. I guess that works both ways. In trade for some bulldozing and planting, Kirk placed a couple of bowhunters on my place. They took no deer on my farm, but they saw several bucks, including a heavy-antlered seven-pointer they photographed. I never saw the buck before rifle season, but I saw other nice ones, including the two I saw with Mom and Aunt Betty. I was sure the opening of rifle season would quickly bring good things.

A "SOONER" WHITETAIL

In mid-November I drove down to Enid, Oklahoma, for the Grand National Quail Hunt, a fun event I try not to miss. No, I didn't win it this year. The birds were there, and we had a great hunt, but I wasn't on my game. I did get a huge bonus: My friends Joey Meibergen and his dad, Butch, invited me to stick around for the opening weekend of the Oklahoma deer season. With an online license in hand, I was all over it.

We hunted near Fort Supply, west of Enid. This is the country of big sand hills and thickets of wild plum and Chinaberry, great for bobwhites and not bad for whitetails. With the rut in full swing, I was expecting a fine opening morning, but we woke up to fog so thick there was no visibility at all. Joey placed me atop a strategic sand hill, finding it only through the magic of GPS, then he felt his way on to the west through the fog and dark. I sat and shivered, hoping the fog would lift at dawn. It did not; I could see nothing for that first critical hour. To my right and left were Chinaberry thickets, with my hill sloping down to a brushy valley, then rising again to a ridge system 400 yards to my front. However, all of this perfect ground was lost in the fog.

About half-past eight I got my first glimpse of the distant ridge, clear enough to see a doe coming through a saddle and immediately bed down. Perfect, a live decoy. The fog came and went along the ridge top, and just a few minutes later I saw a decent eight-pointer on the crest to the right of the doe. The distance was possible, but I had no idea what lay in the valley beyond, so it wasn't a safe shot. I watched, hoping he might come my way, but he stayed on the spine of the ridge, then dropped to the back side and was gone. I was so focused on the buck, I almost didn't see the bigger one on the left-hand ridge.

He stood silhouetted against fog for a few moments, then walked down the ridge in my direction. By now the rifle was well rested and steady. I was hoping he'd come a

Before rifle season, the author saw several better bucks, but post-rut, a full moon and warm weather sent them to ground. On the last night, after 10 days, this mature seven-pointer became his first buck on his own place. The rifle is a custom 7x57 firing 139-grain bullets.
Photo Credit: Craig Boddington

whole lot closer. The fog swirled in, and I lost him for long seconds, then picked him up again at something over 300 yards. He had turned now, and it looked like he was going to go over the ridge to the left. Once he got to the crest there would be no shot, so this was the time. A backline hold seemed about right, and the bullet hit with a tremendous *crack*. Through both recoil and fog I lost the deer completely and had to switch to binoculars to catch him rolling down the ridge.

We spent the rest of the weekend trying to get Joey on a good buck, and we found a dandy, but he gave us the slip in a maze of sandhill draws. So I drove back to Kansas reflecting on my luck—and hoping it would carry through to the Kansas rifle season.

DECEMBER
When rifle season started on Decem-

ber 2nd, it was a given the rut would be over. Strike one. The moon was absolutely full. Strike two. Serious weather would help, but it was mild and clear. Strike three and you're out. Mornings were absolutely dead, with most deer probably bedded by the wee hours. There was random midday movement, and the evenings were pretty good...for does and young bucks. The big boys evaporated, as only big whitetails can.

Under the conditions, this was predictable. I set up a tripod stand hoping to catch the big 10-pointer, but it wasn't shocking I didn't see him. In the search I also took myself out of the primary traffic pattern I'd created with my food plot, so I saw few deer the first part of the season. Donna and Jim had that area to themselves, and they saw several bucks. Three days into the season, with no activity where I was hunting and no shooting going on among my hunting partners, we switched things around a bit.

Yes, there were plenty of deer around. One morning I sat a ladder stand up in the woods while Jim guarded the food plot. I saw a dozen does and three different bucks, but all were little guys. Jim never saw a deer on the wheat field. With his time running short, I moved the tripod toward my northern boundary, overlooking a trail intersection.

I think it was that evening that Donna and I sat on the food plot and had two bucks come out that I'd never seen before—a pretty good eight-pointer and a wide seven-point buck with a bad limp. Both were young deer, but we talked about taking Limpy, then decided not to. He had a big problem with one shoulder, but he was eating and looked in good shape, so we passed. From the tripod Jim saw a spike and a buck with a broken beam, so it seemed to be a good spot. I guess it was; the next morning—his last—he shot a medium-size eight-pointer.

That was the last antler we saw for five long days. Ours is not a big place. Some of the neighbors hunt, and there's public land not far away, along the Elk River. On opening day— a Wednesday—we heard a lot of shooting. It dropped off until the weekend, then picked up a bit. Primary deer tags are either sex, so I took some consolation in believing much of the shooting was at does for the freezer. For sure it was a slow season, with few bucks taken in my neighborhood and the local outfitters reporting slow movement. As the days passed, I wondered what in the world was going on. Had any of the bucks I'd seen survived the opening-day fusillade?

We stayed at it, now concentrating on the food plot. Morning movement stayed slow, but in the late afternoon we averaged 20 does and yearlings. There almost had to be secondary rut activity sooner or later, and even if there wasn't, a cold front did finally come in. By then, time was running out. On our next-to-last evening Donna and I sat until black dark and counted 22 does and fawns, plus one cheeky spike. Even in our cozy blind we just about froze, and on the last evening Donna sensibly decided her time would be better spent packing.

I was a bit late getting into the blind that afternoon and spooked four does. My well-nibbled field of winter wheat was completely empty when, at 4:15, a nice eight-pointer strode into the field. He was not the kind of buck I was hoping for, nor the kind of buck I'd seen. However, he was there, and I'll admit I badly wanted to take a buck during this first season on our own place. If I shot him, he would be the first buck in my life I could take on my own land, in a situation I had worked hard to create. I wrestled with myself, alternating between crosshairs, camera and binoculars. The crosshairs almost won. He was big enough, but I just couldn't make him grow old enough. So I put down the rifle and picked up the camera as he walked back toward the woods.

He stopped at the edge, stared at the blind, then swung his head the other way, along the tree line. Just over the top of his head was another set of antlers. A different buck paused at the edge of the woods, only his head showing. This was a better buck—heavier, wider, taller—and from his face, he was a good deal older. That's as far as I looked. I'd already traded the camera for the binoculars, and now I traded the binoculars for the rifle. Whatever else this buck might be, he was a great gift.

Through the scope I could see just a bit of shoulder, and that's where I put the SST bullet from my 7x57. He ran straight forward across open ground into a little neck of timber, and I saw him go down just beyond the edge. I shot my first deer 45 years ago, and there have been many since, but as I walked to my first deer taken on my own farm, my hands shook uncontrollably. Only when I got to him did I recognize him. He was the old seven-pointer Kirk's bowhunter had photographed in that field fully a month earlier. I have no idea where he'd been hiding all that time, but I hope most of the bucks I saw while scouting were hiding with him. Maybe they'll be a bit bigger next year. ⓗ

LAYNE SIMPSON

493 DEAD DEER

As you may have noticed, most of what I write for this publication is on shotguns, and while I thoroughly enjoy them, my true love is rifles— always has been, and always will be. The first firearm I called my own was a shotgun because that's what my father bought for me, but the first two firearms I purchased with my own money were rifles. I love hunting, too, but unlike some hunters who consider a rifle nothing more than a tool, I enjoy what I am hunting with as much as what I'm hunting. There are those who buy a particular rifle because it's what they need for a particular hunt, but I've been known to buy one and then come up with a hunt for it. Knowing this, it should be easy to understand why I always consider it a pleasure to spend time in the field with someone who shares my passion for the technical side of rifles, cartridges, bullets, scopes and everything else that goes along with them.

Hayward Simmons is that kind of guy. I first hunted whitetails with him more than 20 years ago, about five years after he hung out his shingle as an outfitter in South Carolina. During that hunt we probably talked more about deer rifles than deer hunting, so it was obvious that I was not the only rifle nut in camp. The year was 1988, and I was hunting with the first rifle ever built in a wildcat I had just come up with called the 7mm STW. As I recall, Hayward's favorite rifle at the time was a custom job in .243 Improved called Miss Piggy.

I had the pleasure of hunting with Hayward for several years, and then, as all too often happens with friends, we drifted off in our own directions. The years flew by like leaves pushed along by the wind. Then January of a recent year found me itching all over to hunt deer with a new rifle. Some of the longest days you will ever spend are those that drag along between the time you buy a new rifle and the time you first get to hunt with it. I just couldn't see scratching the itch until October. Deer season opens on August 15 in South Carolina, so I booked a hunt with Hayward Simmons, partially to satisfy the new rifle itch

WHICH CALIBERS & BULLETS ARE THE BEST?

but mostly because I had not hunted with him in many years and we had a lot of catching up to do.

I have often described opening week of the South Carolina season as the most difficult and challenging deer hunting you will find anywhere, and someday I will tell that story as well. In the meantime, this story is about a journal kept by Hayward Simmons on 493 deer killed by his hunters.

It is not unusual for an outfitter to keep written tabs on the number of animals taken, but Hayward has gone far beyond that by recording what cartridge and bullet was used by each hunter, where the bullet struck the deer, how far the animal traveled after it was shot and other interesting information. But before getting into his data, let's first take a brief look at who took those deer and the methods used to harvest them.

Hayward has scaled back his operation considerably during the past few years, but there was a time when he hunted thousands of acres. Deer season in the county in which he operates runs from August 15 through the end of December, and in certain areas and at certain times, it is legal to take both does and bucks, with no limit on the number of bucks taken.

Deer don't grow as large in South Carolina as in states farther north, but it is not unusual for a mature buck to field-dress at 180 pounds or so. Most of the deer shot at Cedar Knoll Plantation are taken from elevated blinds positioned along the edges of cultivated fields or large food plots, most of which are surrounded by thick, brushy terrain and swampy areas. I've taken a few deer from those stands, and it's about like shooting from a benchrest.

According to Hayward's journal, some deer were taken closer and others were farther away when shot, but the average range was 132 yards. Out to about 150 yards most deer shot at were bagged, but as the range increased, so did the number of misses. As for ammunition expended, 603 rounds were used to bump off 493 deer, for an average of 1.22 cartridges per animal. (That figure is actually a bit off, since a few of the rounds fired were finishing shots on wounded deer.) Any way you look at it, 82 percent kills is darned good.

Fifty-one percent of the deer that were shot dropped where they stood, while the rest ran various distances before dropping, with the average being 62 yards. Interestingly, complete misses were slightly higher among female hunters, but the deer shot by them averaged running only 44½ yards before dropping. As Hayward speculates, women are usually less shaken by the sudden appearance of antlers, and that calmness gives them the patience to wait until the target is in

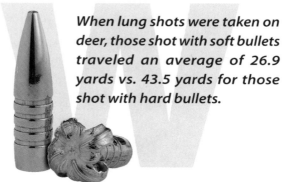

When lung shots were taken on deer, those shot with soft bullets traveled an average of 26.9 yards vs. 43.5 yards for those shot with hard bullets.

the right position for a killing shot. He also believes that cartridge choice is another influencing factor. Women often go for smaller calibers, and a lower level of recoil enables most of them to shoot more accurately. Regardless of the cartridge used, of the deer that ran off after being shot, 28 percent showed no visible signs of being hit.

I grew up hunting in areas of the Southeast where a wounded deer that runs only a short distance into a cottonmouth-infested swamp can be quite difficult to recover. It did not take me long to figure out that a buck shot in the lung area can make quite a few more tracks before expiring, so I switched to the shoulder shot, with positive results. When hunting in more open country, I still often aim for the lung area because it spoils less of the eating part. But anytime I need to drop deer quickly I go for the shoulder.

I found it interesting that Hayward's kill data agreed with my experiences. The average distance

covered by a shoulder-shot deer was only 2.6 yards, compared with 50.4 yards for heart shots and 38.6 yards for shots higher up and through both lungs. The majority of animals shot through the shoulders dropped in their tracks, and most of those that didn't stayed within sight of the hunter. As Hayward put it, the shoulder area is a big target, offering room for error in bullet placement—a bit high cuts major arteries to the heart, and even higher strikes the spine. A bit low gets the heart, and a bullet placed a bit too far back is still in the lungs rather than the guts. His definition of a shot to the shoulder is holding the juncture of the crosshairs in line with the center of the leg and anywhere from a third to halfway up the body from the brisket.

Then we have the matter of rifles and ammunition. Historically, a fairly large percentage of the hunters at Cedar Knoll use rifles custom-built for accuracy, and they also handload. The difference between that group and hunters who stuck with an off-the-shelf rifle and ammo was not great, but it was enough to be noteworthy.

Those who shot handloads in custom rifles killed 88½ deer for every 100 rounds fired, while those who shot factory fodder and rifles averaged 73.2 percent. While not addressed in the data, I tend to believe that the difference had more to do with shooter proficiency than with any performance difference in rifles and ammunition at the ranges at which deer were shot. As a rule, hunters who handload their ammo burn up more rounds in practice than those who shoot factory loads, and we all know that the more a rifle is shot, the more proficient its owner usually becomes.

Differences in cartridge performance will likely surprise a few people. The caliber categories and percentages of the 493 deer that fell victim to them were .243 (11 percent), .25 (8 percent), 6.5mm/.270 (19 percent), 7mm (36 percent) and .30 (26 percent). Clear winners in the killing department were the .25 calibers, which included the .25-06, .257 Roberts, .257 Weatherby Magnum, .257 Ackley Improved, .25-284 and .250 Savage. After being shot with those cartridges, deer ran an average of 14 yards before dropping, compared with 26 yards for various .28 calibers ranging from the 7mm-08 Remington to several 7mm Magnums.

In third place, at an average of 31 yards, were cartridges of 6.5mm and .27 caliber, with the .270 Winchester being the most popular. Bringing up the rear with an average stop distance of 33 yards were various .30 calibers ranging from the .308 Winchester to the .300 Magnums.

From a realistic point of view, the mere seven-yard difference separating the second-, third- and fourth-place cartridge groups is so small that it would be accurate to say that any cartridge in those groups is as effective on deer as the others. But the fact that deer shot with the .25-caliber cartridges traveled only half as far as those shot with the .270 Winchester is something to take note of. In my opinion, the .25s came out on top, not because they are better deer cartridges but because their mild levels of recoil make them easier for many hunters to shoot accurately. To me, the big mystery here are cartridges of 6mm caliber, mainly the .243 Winchester and 6mm Remington. Deer shot with them averaged 41 yards before expiring, and while that's not significantly farther than those shot with various .30-caliber cartridges, both Hayward and I are at a loss to explain why they did not rank closer in performance to cartridges of .25 caliber.

Last but most certainly not least in importance are the bullets used. Hayward separated bullets into two groups, with the Remington Core-Lokt, Federal Power-Shok, Winchester Power-Point, Nosler Ballistic Tip, Sierra Pro-Hunter, Hornady InterLock and Speer softnose classified as "soft," while so-called premium-grade bullets of extreme controlled-expansion construction were lumped into the "hard" category. When lung shots were taken on deer, those shot with soft bullets traveled an average of 26.9 yards vs. 43.5 yards for those shot with hard bullets. This is due to the fact that a soft bullet usually expands to a larger frontal area and, in doing so, destroys a greater amount of tissue, causing more severe internal bleeding. Soft bullets also performed better on shoulder shots, but the difference was not as great as with shots to the lungs. With regard to that last sentence, keep game size in mind. While soft bullets and shoulder shots are a proven combination on small- to medium-size deer, using a bullet of tougher construction is a good idea on big deer and most certainly is the way to go on larger game such as moose and elk.

The kill data compiled by Hayward Simmons may not agree in total with the experiences of other hunters in other parts of the country, but you have to admit that it's difficult to argue with 493 dead deer. Ⓗ

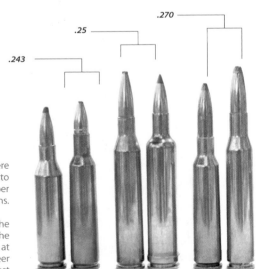

.243   .25   .270   .284   .30

Cartridges were separated into five main caliber classifications.

For this test the .25 class was the most effective at dropping deer in the shortest distance.

FORGET THE GLOOM AND DOOM OF MODERN TIMES. YEAH, WE KNOW THE STOCK MARKET IS DOWN AND UNEMPLOYMENT IS UP, BUT LUCKILY, THE DEER ARE UNAWARE OF OUR DESPERATE NEED TO FILL

The RuT

THE FREEZER WITH MEAT AND WALLS WITH ANTLERS. SO GET IN THE WOODS. YOUR BEST CHANCE AT A TROPHY WHITETAIL IS NOW.

DON'T SCREW IT UP.

The RuT

FAVE F5VE

MIND GAMES

The hardest thing about killing a deer you really want is beating buck fever. But the truth is, the more killing you do, the better you get at it. Most hunters pass up doe after doe waiting for that huge buck and then miss it. Why? Because they haven't shot enough real deer, just targets. Shooting actual deer is the only way to build that instinct within you.

When a buck comes that you do really want, remember that your heart is going to beat fast, your adrenaline will rush and you'll get out of breath—just like when you're about to kiss a girl you really like for the first time. Here's a good way to prepare for and overcome target panic.

Put your bow on a stand where you would normally shoot, walk to your target, then run to your bow, pick it up and shoot within four seconds. If you have several targets, put them at various distances—maybe 40, 30 and 20 yards. Start running from the farthest target first, and shoot at the closest. Alternate targets every time you run and when you shoot. You're going to be breathing heavy and maybe even hyperventilating depending on how many Krispy Kremes you've been eating, but this is a good, cheap simulator to show you how your body will react when excited. As your shooting improves, the better prepared you'll be when the time to crush a real trophy rolls around. —*Michael Waddell*

PICKING THE FIVE BEST deer rifles is an exercise in self-flagellation that's bound to win you few friends and make you a whole lot of enemies. But here it goes anyway.

REMINGTON MODEL 7600 .30-06

Deer hunters in the Northeast know nothing beats a fast, accurate pump gun for tracking elusive whitetails. The Amish Automatic has a reputation for beating up the shoulder, but you won't notice that when racking a second shot into the chamber for a lightning-fast follow-up shot at a gray ghost. There are probably more of these rifles in the Pennsylvania woods on opening day than any other gun. REMINGTON.COM

WINCHESTER MODEL 70 FEATHERWEIGHT .270

A sentimental favorite and my first deer rifle, bought used on the meager income of my first post-college job. Like anyone in his mid-20s, I was shallow, falling as much for the rifle's beautiful lines, including a sexy Schnabel-style fore-end, as for its reputation for accuracy. Luckily, I ended up with both. This is the classic bolt gun that inhabits deer hunters' dreams.

WINCHESTERGUNS.COM

WEATHERBY MARK V DELUXE & ACCUMARK .257

I liken Weatherby owners to those parents whose kids are standout star athletes. They won't shut up about them, and they're always showing you pictures of their latest achievements. But then, if your kid were shooting sub-MOA groups, you'd be doing the same. The Mark V is that star quarterback, albeit with a funky Monte Carlo stock. And when you reach out there and touch some whitetail from afar, follow the advice of some of history's great coaches: Act like you've been there before.

WEATHERBY.COM

MARLIN 336 .30-30

Whether or not the venerable .30-30 has killed more deer than any other cartridge is an argument for another article, but either way, it's a classic. Winchester started the lever-gun revolution with the 1894, but Marlin perfected it in the 336. Its real advantage is the flattop receiver that accommodates a scope, something Winchester didn't figure out until the early '80s.

MARLINFIREARMS.COM

4 DEER DEATH ZONES

Focus on these **top four** critical terrain features common to virtually anywhere in whitetail country and setup for the ultimate rut-time ambush.

Oak Flats and Ridges—Whether running down the spine of a big woods ridge top or parked squarely in the middle of some remote tangle of flatlands forest, a buck's mind may not be on food right now, but like Kirstie Alley passing a Dunkin Donuts, you can bet the girls' thoughts are. Walk the perimeter of these open-woods smorgasbords and you'll likely find a nasty rub line indicating where bucks are cruising the locale looking for action. Hang a stand where prevailing winds will cast your scent away from the scrape line and acorn-strewn ground, and be there well before sun-up. These spots are best in early mornings as bucks cruise in search of does returning from the nighttime fields.

Creek Bottoms—When guns start booming, deer feel the pressure and retreat to cover even as the need to breed urges them on. Brush-choked creek bottoms carved into the landscape and tree-lined streamside management zones (SMZs to the initiated) lining through clear-cut terrain provide natural whitetail highways where does and trailing bucks cruise under cover. Tall-growing water-fed trees make for great perches on which to hang a stand. Find crossings where hooves have cleaved away the soil on both sides of the creek and mud worn trails paralleling the banks, and plan to spend the day on stand.

ROCK RIVER LAR-8 .308

Here's where the old-timers will stop reading and all our servicemen give out a "Hell yeah!" Fact is, the AR platform—or modern sporting rifle, as we're supposed to call it—has its place in the deer woods, and here's my unconventional argument why: It's a great gun for young shooters. That's right, I said it. Equipped with an adjustable stock, the AR's length of pull grows as the shooter does. And the .308 Winchester cartridge, when shot through a gas-operated semiauto, is a great cartridge that packs a punch, without punching the shooter in the shoulder. Also available in a 6.8 SPC version! **ROCKRIVERARMS.COM** —*David Draper*

Remote Fields—Often reserved for evening hunts only, an open field, whether big and sporting a season's stubble of cut corn or beans or small and revealing the lush green of a well-planted food plot, is hard to resist morning, midday or afternoon during the rut. But don't waste time on roadside fields where every pickup truck slows at the sight of a grazing whitetail. Deer will quickly learn to avoid such spots, and you should, too. Find a remote opening or field, and leave it alone for at least two weeks up to the rut, then hit it when the action turns on. Set up 10 to 20 yards inside the edge, as bucks are more apt to cruise the inside line of woods looking for field-feeding does than stroll right into the open. That being said, be ready for anything. When you least expect it, a big boy still may bust midfield. Be sure you have a shooting lane or two clear to the open.

Funnels—No matter where you hunt, any terrain feature that narrows deer movement into a predictable location where you can set a stand and make a shot is going to be your best bet. Bucks are on the move this time of year, so you have to play that hand and put yourself in a place where the landscape will force the parade past your setup. A neck or point of woods between two larger lots of trees, hillsides narrowing toward each other, a wide waterway bending in toward a field, converging fence lines, holes or low wires on fences, even a narrow gap between suburban homes—all of these locations provide top spots to hang a stand both when the rut is coming on and when it's in full swing. Scout these areas well, scope out satellite imagery and determine which funnels between the best feed and bedding are likely to produce the best big-buck opportunities.

—*Doug Howlett*

KEEP'EM COMING

Passive hunting is for the weak and lazy. Get proactive in your pursuit of whitetails, and keep using both buck and doe calls throughout the rut.

TYPE OF CALL	TIME OF SEASON	WHEN TO USE	HOW TO USE	TOP MODEL
GRUNT TUBE A deep, burp-like vocalization made by bucks to alert others to their presence, communicate with does and initiate challenges to other bucks.	✓ EARLY SEASON ✓ PRE-RUT ✓ RUT ✓ POST RUT	Sure, you can call blindly with it, but deer aren't ducks. Works best if blown to catch the attention and interest of passing bucks after spotting them first.	A single grunt or two can arouse a buck's curiosity, while a series of two to four grunts can mimic a buck tending or trailing a doe. Use a longer grunt and slower cadence to imitate a buck actively breeding a doe.	**HUNTER'S SPECIALTIES:** TRUE TALKER 2 DEER CALL
DOE BLEAT A high-pitched whine made by does and fawns. Alerts does and bucks to their presence as well as signals readiness to breed.	EARLY SEASON ✓ PRE-RUT ✓ RUT ✓ POST RUT	As area does near estrus, this call announces the willingness to breed. When hunting near good cover, perform a series of bleats every 15 to 20 minutes.	A series of three or four short, quick bleats, used whether or not bucks are in sight, can produce fantastic results.	**PRIMOS:** THE CAN
RATTLING HORNS Imitates two bucks fighting or sparring for dominance.	EARLY SEASON ✓ PRE-RUT ✓ RUT POST RUT	Blind rattling will grab the attention of nearby bucks and bring them in.	Every 15 to 30 minutes give a rattling sequence. If you have visual on a buck, use just enough to keep him coming.	**KNIGHT & HALE:** PACK RACK
SNORT WHEEZE A challenging blow made by bucks.	EARLY SEASON PRE-RUT ✓ RUT POST RUT	A short challenge call given to a dominant buck.	Best if blown to an aggressive, dominant buck.	**M.A.D. CALLS:** HYPER-GROWL

FAST STRIKE

TACTICS

Accessing a likely big-buck hangout must be done with stealth. Remember the following so you don't blow a monster out of the area before you even climb into your stand.

• Practice climbing with or putting up your stand until you can do it quickly and, most important, quietly. Hanging a stand next to a key bedding area is no time to figure out how it goes together.

• When putting up a lock-on stand, do it at night, where deer won't associate your presence with daytime hunt activity.

• Scout likely areas you might want to hit before the rut kicks in. Mark possible stand trees with survey tape so you are not wandering around looking for that perfect tree hours or even moments before you plan to hunt the area.

• Use rubber boots in shallow creeks, existing trails and field edges with barren soil whenever possible to access an area as silently and scent-free as possible. Wear smaller-soled, lightweight boots or tennis shoes for quieter walking. If you need heavier boots for warmth, tie them to your pack or stand while walking in and put them on in the stand. —*Doug Howlett*

TAKING THE SHOT

While every situation is different, here are a few techniques/ rules and observations I have found helpful when taking the shot.

~ As soon as I see a deer coming, I get my bow in hand and my rangefinder ready. I don't like to be caught off guard when a big boy steps out.

~ If a group of deer have been going along the same trail and moved a certain way, the buck you are looking at now will probably do the same thing. If their movement presented better shots down the trail, wait. If not, now might be your only chance.

~ Deer will occasionally look up and catch movement, but for the most part they are generally preoccupied, and as long as you move slowly, you will be fine. However, if the deer is getting ultra close, you can wait for him to step behind a tree where his head is hidden before moving.

~ It is almost impossible to draw your bow without making noise, and on a really quiet day, there is a good chance that a deer will hear the sound of you drawing. In these cases, wait to draw when the buck enters a wide shooting lane. —*Michael Waddell*

WREAK DECOY DEVASTATION

...ecoys for the deer rut? It may seem unnecessary or even burdensome, ...ut the right decoy in the right setup can seal the deal during the rut ...d bring that pursuing buck to within a stone's throw.

...hen to Use: The best time to bust out a decoy starts when bucks ...gin hierarchy posturing through the active breeding of does.

...here to Place It: Travel routes between bedding and feeding areas ...esent the safest endeavor with the most opportunities to encounter ...ultiple bucks. Fields and food plots are a good evening location. If ...u can get near bedding areas without getting busted, a territory-...fringing decoy can be deadly.

...ost Important: Perhaps more important than what type of area ...u place a decoy in is how visible it is. Place it in heavy cover and ...u might as well have left it at home. Visibility is the key. It's a visual ...tractor that needs to be seen in order to be effective.

...ositioning: An investigating buck might circle downwind of the ...ecoy to try and cut the fake's scent. He'll also approach a buck decoy ...ad-on, challenging and posturing for a fight. Keep those two things ...mind during placement, and be sure that downwind route he might ...llow won't put you where you can be winded.

...hich Sex? If you can tote both a buck and doe decoy into the woods, ...u double the chances of infuriating a passing buck. If you can only ...oose one, go with a buck early in the pre-rut and switch to a doe ...ter in the season. A lone buck might anger a territorial male into ...ghting earlier on, but the longer the rut continues and the more ...oes available to breed, the less likely he'll bother with fighting once ...eeding is taking place.

...d Realism: Slapping a decoy out in the open and just sitting on ...ur butt isn't going to work. Use grunts or bleats to get a passing ...uck's attention. Once he looks your way and identifies the decoy as ...possible intruder or mate, ease off the calls and let the visual cue ...ork. If he's hanging up, work the grunt tube to anger him and perhaps ...eak out the snort-wheeze if necessary. With doe decoys, slap on a ...tle estrous scent. —*Brian Lynn*

SLUG GUNS VS. SMOKEPOLES

IN MANY STATES WHERE DEER seasons are commonly known as "shotgun only," hunters actually have the option of using either a slug-loaded shotgun or a muzzleloader. Either will do the job, but each has its evangelists, spreading the gospel on why its gun of choice is *The One*. Here's an unbiased look at which might be right for you.

Shotguns—Slug gun accuracy has come a long way in recent years as ammo manufacturers have shrunk groups with advancements in slug and sabot technologies. But with those advancements come higher costs. Top-shelf ammo can set a shooter back up to $20 or more per five-round box. And if that hurts the wallet, just think what a 12-gauge 3½-inch load is going to do to your shoulder. That's why many guys opt for a 20-gauge, which delivers ample energy downrange and is deadly accurate. No longer limited to 50-yard shots, the right barrel, load and scope combo can achieve pie-plate or better accuracy out past 150. And don't forget fast follow-up shots, which make the shotgun ideal for traditional deer drives.

Muzzleloaders—"Shotgun" season is the only time frontstuffers can't be called the traditional choice. For most gun hunters, "muzzleloader" means "modern inlines," and that equals MOA accuracy out to 200 yards and beyond. Sure, you're sacrificing a quick follow-up shot, but if you've put in your bench work, you shouldn't need it. After the initial sticker shock of a rifle/scope combo, you'll save on per-shot cost, which is priced in cents rather than double-digit dollars. A great choice for stand or still hunters who want one-shot accuracy at longer ranges, modern muzzleloaders are the closest thing deer hunters can get to a modern rifle in shotgun-only season. —*David Draper*

POST-RUT IN KANSAS

CRAIG BODDINGTON

EVERY DEER SEASON BRINGS NEW LESSONS.

It was about 7:30 on a bitter morning, and a bit of pale light was starting to creep through the tall oaks. I was in a high ladder stand, shivering almost uncontrollably. I was hunting a ridge on my little place in southern Kansas, so these were my oaks, and I was hunting my deer. As I've written before, this is a special thrill that's actually fairly new to me. But at this moment I wasn't thrilled. I was cold, and I was also frustrated. This was the fourth morning of our too-short rifle season, and I hadn't yet seen an antler.

Then I heard a rustle in the leaves behind me, and suddenly I wasn't cold anymore. I swiveled my eyes as far as they would go—not far enough—so I followed slowly with my head and neck. Two does passed behind me, picking their way through the noisy carpet. One of them kept looking behind her, and sure enough, a young eight-pointer followed. I didn't want him, and a good thing that was ... left-handed me would have to stand and turn clear around. The buck was less than 20 yards away, so there was little chance of getting away with all that movement.

No problem. I watched him amble along behind the does, rustling for acorns as he went. When they were gone I slowly turned back, only to find another, smaller buck crossing to my front. Thus began a most incredible parade. In the next half hour eight more bucks and an undetermined number of does and fawns crossed my ridge. Most were youngsters, but two were reasonable ten-pointers. One was probably 3½ years old, the larger of the two possibly a year older. He rooted around almost under my stand, a perfect bow shot. I never raised the rifle, and when there seemed

to be a break in the procession I climbed out of the stand and got the heck out of there.

FOOD SOURCES

Okay, I've never claimed to be a great whitetail hunter, but I've hunted them a lot, and I'm still learning. That morning retaught me an obvious lesson that I supposed I've learned a dozen times. Maybe I'm a slow learner. You see, my little farm is mostly heavy woods, thick oaks that are difficult to hunt. So I cheated. There's a central valley that was once farmed, an ideal place for a food plot. So I bulldozed 20 years of second growth. Okay, "I" is a bit shaky . . . I don't have a clue how to drive a bulldozer! My buddy Kirk Kelso bulldozed it, and in due time I burned the piles and did some of the tractor work (which I'm also not very good at). Fortunately, my neighbors are darned good farmers, so between David Newton, Chuck Herbel, and me we got in a pretty respectable food plot.

Then I cheated some more. In Kansas we're allowed to use feeders, so I put in a great solar-powered feeder from HB Hunting Products. Now, just how might one hunt a

Kansas allows feeders, and Boddington has a good one...but just because you lay a table for the deer doesn't mean they will come to it. At the beginning of the 2010 season, the majority of the deer were in the woods munching acorns.
Photo Credit: Craig Boddington

food plot stretching to 300 yards in a couple of directions? Well, that's easy. I put in a Texas-style tower blind from the same company. It's insulated, so I tell everyone it's Donna's stand. Truth is, I hate sitting in the cold as much as she does!

The stand is set properly with the prevailing wind, right at the corner of the field, so it can be accessed quietly and secretly in the dark. Now, with a situation like that, it offers an almost irresistible hunting option . . . maybe too irresistible. Deer were hitting the wheat field, and there were plenty of tracks around the feeder. We had some friends from California in the first week of season, John and Judy Sonne. John had never hunted

whitetail, so of course I put him in the best place . . . over the food plot. I wasn't about to shoot a deer until he did, so I sat with him a couple of mornings and evenings.

We had a few does and fawns on the food plot every morning and every evening, but the first three days of the season passed without sight of a single antler. I was perplexed. There are a few good bucks in the neighborhood, but there are lots of young and medium-sized bucks. The moon was wrong and opening day was warm, so I figured the rut had more or less shut down and most movement was nocturnal. But it still didn't make sense.

Well, it made plenty of sense to the deer . . . I just wasn't thinking

He was not the biggest buck we knew about, not even close. For three years now there's been a typical 12-POINTER IN THE AREA, a giant of a deer that several neighbors have seen.

like they were. We'd had a record acorn crop, and as long as the acorns lasted they couldn't care less about all the goodies I'd laid out for them! On the fourth morning, Saturday, I finally smartened up and headed to the woods . . . and I found the deer.

INTO THE WOODS

That afternoon I put John in the stand where I'd been, and I went to a stand on a lower ridge near my east boundary. This area is a natural funnel, still heavy oaks but hidden rimrock on top, with several major trails intersecting. John saw several does and some of the smaller bucks I'd seen, but none of the bigger bucks I'd seen in the morning. It was a quieter afternoon for me, but a full hour before dark I saw what appeared to be a really good buck slipping along behind two does. I had never seen this buck before, and I didn't see him well. I thought he was a very big eight-pointer, but he could have carried more. Whatever the points, he had heavy beams, with good height and lots of width.

This time I was tempted. I got the rifle up and the crosshairs on him, but managed to resist. He was headed from some heavy bedding cover toward a nearby CRP, pretty normal movement. So on Sunday morning we switched, me hoping that same buck would work his way back onto my place and show up for John.

I took the stand on the big ridge again . . . and was treated to the same procession of bucks. I'm pretty sure I didn't see the largest ten-pointer, but I saw most of the same bucks again plus a couple of differ-

Boddington's buck quickly proved to be heavier than it looked. Fortunately, his daughter, Brittany, was close at hand to help drag it out of the woods.

Photo Credit: Craig Boddington

ent ones. Honestly, I haven't yet figured out why the bucks like that particular ridge, but clearly they do. Once again, I had no intention of shooting... well, not unless I saw a real monster. But I enjoyed the morning, and as is normal on a weekend in deer season, I heard a few scattered shots.

Sound plays strange games among the big oaks. I heard a couple of reports that might have been John, but I wasn't sure until I met him on the road and saw blood on his hands. Then I raced up to him so I could see which deer he'd shot.

A POST-RUT SEASON

It's a funny thing. My place is in a network of smaller farms, so nobody owns the deer. I have great bedding cover, but some of the neighbors have better feed, including some

farming areas. So the deer come and go. All the neighbors hunt deer at least a little bit, but nobody is a really serious trophy hunter ... we just hunt deer, although I suppose we all hope for the best. By the time rifle season rolls around there's a pretty good collective knowledge of what the year's crop looks like.

Whitetails being whitetails, there are bucks that we don't know about, but there are usually a few distinctive "known" bucks. John shot one of them, an ancient, monstrous six-pointer, a true trophy buck in terms of age, spread, mass, and length . . . he just didn't have the points, although he might have in previous years. I had never seen that buck, but neighbor David Newton had described him—and intended to shoot him if he got the chance. Well, I'd have shot him, too, but he came by John's stand a little past eight.

He was not the biggest buck we knew about, not even close. For three years now there's been a typical 12-pointer in the area, a giant of a deer that several neighbors have seen. Except he's never been seen when rifle season was open. The previous season I saw two different and very nice 10-pointers . . . but neither buck was seen during the 2011 season. That good buck I saw Saturday afternoon, well, that's the only time I saw him.

This is all par for the course with a post-rut season, which is what we have to contend with. It was set up that way back in the Sixties, when Kansas held its first modern deer season. Back then, when we had far fewer deer, the theory was to give every buck a chance to breed before hunting season. It has been that way ever since, and there seems little likelihood of a change. Our deer

generally rut in November, and that's archery season. Bowhunters thus have a tremendous advantage and take at least their fair share of the big Kansas bucks we all dream about. The advantage is extreme enough that I may wind up taking up the bow again (just don't tell anybody).

Post-rut hunting is more difficult. Many of the big bucks go completely nocturnal; others are all broken up from fighting. Traditionally, the rifle season opens the Wednesday after Thanksgiving. This is early enough to catch the tail end of the rut, so what we really hope for is weather. If it gets cold we get pretty good movement. If it doesn't, well, it's tough. In the 2010 season I'm writing about, opening day was warm with a full moon, which couldn't be worse. Well, that's not true. I made it worse by hunting fields rather than woods the first few days!

By the weekend, when John shot his buck, temperatures dropped way down, and we had reasonable movement for the rest of the season. Understand, however, that frantic rutting activity was long since over. During the post-rut you can expect a lot of nocturnal movement, which you can't do much about. You can figure out what the deer are eating, and you can figure out where they're bedding. Others might do differently, but I stay out of the bedding grounds. The carpet of leaves is so heavy that quiet movement is impossible, and my place is small enough that all I'm likely to do is push the deer away.

The ultimate dream would be a foot of new snow on opening day, and then look out! Failing that, we leave the core bedding cover alone and hunt either feeding areas or movement corridors between bedding grounds and feed. This works, except that I know we have bigger bucks than we see . . . I just haven't yet figured out what to do about it!

FOOD CHOICES CHANGE

At the beginning of the 2010 season the deer were on acorns, and I should have figured that out sooner than I did. This sounds elementary, my dear Watson, and it really is . . . but I had a lot of time, effort, and some cash invested in my fine food plot setup, and I was too reluctant to abandon it. Dumb. On the other hand, things can change fast. We had so many acorns that I don't think they ran out, but after several days of heavy frost—by the seventh day of the season—it seems the acorns went bad. The deer were back on the open fields, including my food plot.

At the end of the season things sort of went back to normal, with up to two dozen does and yearlings on the wheat every evening. By then the moon was getting dark, which helped, but morning traffic was sporadic, and typical of post-rut conditions, the bucks were much more nocturnal than the does.

Because so much movement was in the thick woods, it was a tough season in my area, notable by the lack of shots heard, but

toward the tail end, bucks started making last-light appearances. On the second Wednesday a nice buck was missed in my food plot, and on the last weekend, I turned it over to David Newton. He had two grandkids trying to get their first deer. This normally wouldn't be a problem, but he needed a setup where they could be coached, and my comfy stand provided a good solution. They got their deer, and so ended the 2010 season.

DECISION TIME

By then I was long since done. Having learned my lesson, I stayed in the woods, alternating between three different stands, depending on the wind. I think it was Tuesday morning, and I was in the same ladder stand where John shot his deer. A couple of does passed in front of me early, and it was nearly nine o'clock when I heard a rustle behind me. I thought it was an armadillo—they make a terrible ruckus in the leaves—but I looked around and

saw a flash of brown in some really thick stuff down the ridge.

I picked out a doe, then another, and then a third . . . and then just a quick flash of antler behind them. The deer were maybe 75 yards away, just at the limit of my vision, so I stood up slowly and turned around in the stand, thankful for the safety harness. The deer were angling up the ridge, just bits and pieces visible. I never got a proper look at the antlers, but there was some mass and plenty of points. Honestly, I thought it was the same buck I'd seen four days earlier from that stand. This was not correct, but I'd made my decision and now my concern, was how to get a shot. Sprawling backwards across the stand like a spider, I took a rest on the arm support and kept the scope on the shadowed form of the buck. His shoulder came clear for just an instant, and I fired the little 7x57.

Funny, there's nothing that gets me going like a buck deer. I guess it was a long-suppressed childhood fantasy to hunt deer on my own place, because after the shot I found myself shaking like a leaf. After a little bit I calmed down enough to unload the rifle and get out of the stand, and then I went to look for the buck. He wasn't the one I'd thought he was. In fact, he was another buck that I'd never seen before. But he was big enough, and I'm still learning. ⊕

Brittany Boddington and her dad with his 2010 Kansas buck, very average for the area. Seen in thick stuff, this isn't the buck he thought it was, but it's good enough. Boddington used his Todd Ramirez 7x57 with 139-grain Hornady SST bullets.

EARLY SEASON DEER PRIMER

SCORE EARLY, SCORE OFTEN

TRY THESE *SIX* STRATEGIES FOR KILLING DEER EARLY IN THE SEASON.

I love to bow hunt probably more than just about anything, and this is the time of year many of us live for. But we need to approach early season much differently than the rut. Bucks aren't charging around reckless like they will be come November, but that's okay. If we play our cards right, the early season could pay off much better than even the rut, simply because we're getting the first crack at these big boys. Here are six tips that will have you driving a wallhanger home in your truck.

1 SCOUT IT OUT

Even if you've hunted a place a million times, scouting is important. Deer will stick to traditional patterns from year to year. However, food sources change, plots and crop fields might be planted differently, woods get cut, and swamps dry out or flood depending on the rain. All of this can affect where deer are bedding and feeding, the latter being the most important. In the early season, you're going to focus on food sources as bucks try to beef up and prepare for the rut. Identify these spots and hang stands well before the season. Set up trail cams and spend time glassing where deer routinely enter a field or food plot. It's hot, so deer will bed near food, which is everywhere at this time of season, so it's important to have multiple locations pinpointed.

2 KNOW YOUR FOOD

You need to identify all of the potential early season food sources and hunt them as deer hit them. Woods will be greened up meaning there's plenty for bucks to browse; however, they will still seek out the most nutritious foods. If acorns are plentiful, particularly on white oaks, deer will be there when they start dropping over any other food source. Plots planted in clover are good September or early October magnets; however, if agricultural fields of soybeans and corn are nearby, it will trump most small food plots hunters plant, particularly as the weather begins to cool.

3 WATER WONDERS

Deer get a lot of the moisture they need from the late-summer foods they eat, so if you live in an area with abundant flowing streams, flooded swamplands, or near large creeks and rivers, you'll be wasting your time trying to set up along the edge of a creek, hoping to catch a big buck coming to drink. Odds of catching a deer in one drinking spot are thin. But if you hunt in drought-stricken areas such as Texas and Oklahoma or other dry areas, a stock tank or isolated pond can be a great spot to hang a stand. Scout the travel routes around the water source, identify where most of the tracks are made, and set up there to catch an antlered monster coming to the drink.

4 DON'T FORCE IT

A lot of stands are accessed by fields, which is where the deer will be feeding at dawn. If you're hoping to score on a buck as it goes to bed in the morning, but the only practical way you have to get into your stand is through the field where he's likely to be feeding, don't go. Wait and hunt the spot in the afternoon.

5 HOLD YOUR SHOT

Bucks are likely still in bachelor groups the first week or two of most bow seasons. That means you don't want to shoot the first buck that steps into view since a bigger dude might be right behind him. Note the make-up of these groups from trail cam photos and scouting. Identify the one you want in the bunch and try to hit him when he shows up with his buddies to feed. If you see one of his partners, you know your target buck is likely nearby.

6 MAKE AN EVENING EXIT STRATEGY

Remember, if you walked through a field to your stand in the early afternoon, deer will likely be feeding in that same field when it comes time to go. Just blowing out of there after dark can spook that buck you're targeting and run him from the area. Instead, mark an alternate trail that loops you deep through the woods and gets out without going near the field. Or, if nothing else, be prepared to sit tight until it appears deer have fed out of the field and moved on. —*Michael Waddell*

RUGER
AMERICAN

The Ruger American is a price-point rifle that doesn't look or feel like one. The 6¼-pound rifle has a short, 70-degree bolt lift and an attractive synthetic stock with stainless-steel bedding blocks molded right in. Ruger's new Marksman adjustable trigger provides a crisp, three- to five-pound pull, and the free-floated barrel is cold hammer forged. The barrel, trigger, and bedding blocks combine to deliver sub-MOA accuracy at a price most hunters can afford. It is available in .243, .270, .308, .30-06. **$449**

RUGER.COM

MERKEL
RX HELIX

The RX Helix combines Old World beauty with a new straight-pull bolt-action design that is, perhaps, one of the only truly innovative rifle designs to be unveiled this year. The Helix employs a rotating bolt head with six locking lugs. Moving the bolt handle transmits motion to the bolt head at a ratio of two-to-one thanks to a revolutionary transmission gearing system. It cycles silky-smooth and lightning fast. Oh, it's also a takedown. It is available in three action lengths and 12 calibers, from .222 to 9.3x62. Starts at **$3,995**

MERKEL-USA.COM

FAB
4

—Greg Rodriguez

WEATHERBY
VANGUARD SERIES 2

Weatherby's acclaimed Vanguard line just got better, with new models and more features, including a new match-grade, two-stage trigger that is user adjustable to as little as 2.5 pounds. Select models offer a new stock that incorporates the classic high-combed Weatherby style with modern upgrades like Griptonite inserts for enhanced traction in wet weather and a hand-filling palm swell. A bead-blasted finish is now standard, as is a sub-MOA accuracy guarantee. Several finish, barrel length, caliber, and stock options are available. **$549–1,049**

WEATHERBY.COM

T/C
DIMENSION

Thompson/Center's revolutionary Dimension Rifle combines T/C quality with a radically designed synthetic stock and a unique switch-barrel system. The easily interchangeable, Locking Optimized Components (LOC) include the barrel, bolt, magazine, and magazine housing. Each part is lettered from A to D, with each letter corresponding to a family of cartridges, from the poodle-pounding .204 Ruger all the way up to moose-busting .300 Win. Mag. The parts interchange quickly and easily, and the barrels hold their zero because the scope is mounted directly on the barrel instead of the receiver. **$649**

TCARMS.COM

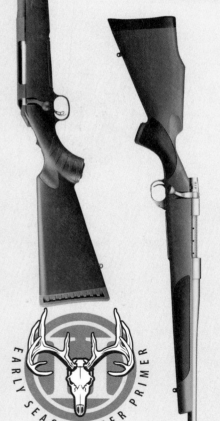

EARLY SEASON DEER PRIMER

Whitetail Sleeper States

THERE IS NO SHORTAGE of ink that has been spilled on the deer hunting and bucks in such trophy destinations as Illinois, Wisconsin, Iowa, and Kansas. Turn on outdoor television and it seems every hunter is scrambling to film a hunt in these states, with thousands of every-day, traveling hunters right on their heels. While all of these states do a great job managing their herds, hunting can fall short of high-dollar expectations when you're not among the first group of the season to hit the woods. And speaking of high dollar, many hunts in these states command some of the highest price tags in deer hunting.

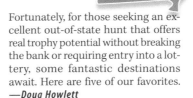

Fortunately, for those seeking an excellent out-of-state hunt that offers real trophy potential without breaking the bank or requiring entry into a lottery, some fantastic destinations await. Here are five of our favorites.
—*Doug Howlett*

Photo Credit: Doug Howlett

MINNESOTA

While Wisconsin's Buffalo County boasts more bucks in the book than any other in the U.S., hunting across the river in Minnesota can be pretty darn good. I tried it out this past fall with Pat Gaffney's RAM Outfitters and had a shot at a monster. I botched the shot. Later on, Gaffney's hunters began stacking up nice bucks, including a 160-plus inch 8-point. Gaffney's hunts are either semi-or self-guided—he gives you a property, takes you to it, and shows you were the stands are. Average cost is $900-$1,500 for four to five days of hunting. That's a lot more affordable than the $5K for Pike County or Iowa hunts. A nonres license is only $140.

NEBRASKA

While its neighbors to the East and South get much of the attention, Nebraska is an emerging frontier state, if you will, where big abundant whitetails, ample land and food, and great opportunity co-exist. Hunters in the state enjoyed a record season in 2010, and last year in the southeastern part of the state Kevin Petrzilka killed a 17-point buck that scored a whopping 202^{6}/$_{8}$, not only setting a new state record for a typical buck, but was also said to be the largest typical whitetail killed anywhere in the country in the last 39 years. Bet that gets you thinking about where you should be hunting this season.

MISSOURI

Dream of hunting Iowa, but didn't draw a tag. On average, a nonresident hunter can expect to draw a tag there every three years if he applies each year. So what's a hunter to do on those off years? Scoot across the state line to the Show Me State of Missouri. There, licenses are over-the-counter, will run you about $225, and much of the land is not unlike that of big buck states Iowa and Illinois. The Missouri Department of Conservation also manages quite a bit of public land for the hunter looking to go on the total cheap. Bow hunters there saw harvest numbers trump the previous year's by a third.

OHIO

After setting a record harvest just two seasons ago, the past two seasons have mellowed some, 2010-2011 because of a super abundance of acorns that made it so deer never had to move from cover and last year due to weird warm weather that seemed to baffle hunters across the country the entire season. That being said, hunters are still killing record-book bucks in the Buckeye State each year. Genetics common to the Midwest are alive and well there. Lengthy seasons that run from September to February, and nonresident licenses that cost a mere $149 make Ohio a state to set your sights on.

EARLY SEASON DEER PRIMER

Get a JUMP
on everyone

Today's world is about immediate gratification, so who can wait until late September or October—or, for some of you gun diehards, all the way until November, God forbid—to enter the deer woods. Two places provide summer deer hunting action while most hunters are still sitting on the beach with the family, yelling at the kids to not drown, sipping a few cold ones, and attempting to sneak a peak through dark shades at the tan Betties walking by without getting busted by the wife. To get in on the action, you have to go coastal; bi-coastal that is.

In the East, South Carolina's Low Country is home to the earliest whitetail season in the nation with an opening date—for both gun and bow—of August 15th. It remains one of the best opportunities in the nation to kill a legitimate whitetail trophy still sporting velvet antlers. Temps in the Palmetto State can soar into the upper 90s at this time of year and the mosquitoes are more bloodthirsty than a pack of Vampires in an Anne Rice novel, but those are the risks you endure for a shot at such a rare trophy.

In the West, California's coastal blacktail season comes in even earlier—if you're a bowhunter—July 15, with gun season traditionally following the second Saturday of August. Famed outdoor writer Craig Boddington, who lives and hunts in the region, notes that Zone A, where the hunting takes place, stretches from Santa Barbara north for several hundred miles. Public land is limited and the hunting tough, but for the locals who pursue these blacktails (some an actual mix with California mule deer) it's a beloved tradition that goes back almost to WWII. —*Doug Howlett*

Photo Credit: Don Jones

Bill Winke

Smells Like Money
Proper scents equal early season pay dirt.

The use of scents is one of the most practiced yet misunderstood tactics in hunting—particularly the early season. Too many hunters, focused on the rut and wanting their scents to bring a big boy running in, roll into the woods during early bow season, as most deer are beginning to spar and break up from bachelor groups, and hang wicks of doe estrous. However, this could be one of the worst things a hunter can do.

"People's expectations of what is going to happen when they dump the pee out of the bottle isn't realistic. It really comes down to using the right scent at the right time," says Mike Mattly with Code Blue Scents. Deer know what smells are natural for that time in the woods, and hunters thinking they are going to fool a buck into believing a doe has come into estrus early will most often find the joke's on them. Most bucks will know something isn't right and bolt.

In fact, before the rut, the best scent may not be a doe-based scent at all.

"A hunter will have better luck in the pre-rut using a buck scent, since dominant bucks are checking scrape lines and getting territorial," he says. By applying buck scent to your setup, you stand a good chance of agitating the buck at this perceived new competitor and can program him to check the area more often to see who is encroaching. The best way to do this is still the ol' mock scrape trick.

First, scout out a few areas where you have seen scrapes in the past or, even better, are already seeing them pop up. Field edges, logging trails, old fence lines through the woods (particularly where there is a gap to funnel deer movement), as well as natural pinch points that force deer past a spot are all good locations. Wearing rubber boots and gloves to minimize human scent, rough up or clear out an 18- to 24-inch circle using a heavy stick beneath a small branch that hangs about 5 feet off the ground. Break the licking branch so about six inches of it hangs loose from the main limb. Deer will lick and rub their heads on these signposts adding more scent to the area.

Pour at least an ounce of buck urine in the scrape. Some hunters like to use a square of wax paper buried just beneath the surface to keep it from seeping away. Keep the scrape fresh with a scent dripper hung above your licking branch. Code Blue also offers Grave Digger Scrape Mate or Grave Digger Whitetail Buck scent impregnated soils that you can mix into the dirt. When accessing the area to hunt, go in as scent free as possible, pulling a drag with buck scent behind. —*Doug Howlett*

10 WAYS

DOUG HOWLETT

TO SCORE BIG IN THE PRE-RUT

DON'T HOLD OUT FOR THE RUT TO TAG YOUR TROPHY THIS SEASON. NOW IS THE TIME TO MAKE THINGS HAPPEN.

I's been a hot, dry across much of the whitetail's range, but the summertime blues have done little to dampen the enthusiasm of deer hunters anticipating the approaching fall. With the first high-mercury days of bow season starting to give way to cool mornings and increasingly-on-the-move bucks, it's time to put your game face on and get serious about the quickly approaching rut. While November is considered primetime for many rut-focused hunters—most of them toting firearms—October is like the special preview for members only, providing serious whitetail chasers with that first true crack at a trophy on the hoof and an opportunity to make this the season of their lifetime before the bulk of hunters have even stepped into the woods. The following tips will give you that edge at this unique time of year and ensure that your chance to jump-start the 2012-2013

2. WORK THE WATER EDGE

With dry conditions predominating much of the weather to this point (see sidebar), isolated ponds, still-wet deeper holes in dried-up swamps or stream beds, a stock tank, and even a small, flowing creek or water-filled ditch can attract deer to stop and drink in the mornings before going off to bed or in the evening before beginning their feed. Scout the water edge to confirm ample hoof marks in the mud and hang a stand within bow range, mindful of prevailing winds in the area. A pond or single isolated water source is easier to target, particularly if surrounded with cover. If a winding creek or ditch is what you have to work with, walk its length, find where the muddiest, most worn deer trails intersect the water, and set your stand off the most visited spot.

1. HUNT FIELDS EARLY

As a buck's attention transitions from feeding to breeding and the summer heat lingers into fall, food will still be on does' minds, which means bucks will still head for the fields. You should, too. These hunts are most productive in the afternoon, and with daylight savings time still in effect, you can still catch quality stand time even after putting in a near full day of work. Soybeans, alfalfa, and peas are great, as is corn if it's cut (or even better, only partially cut with some rows standing), as the availability of high-protein forage will draw deer better than any food plot or natural browse (except maybe white oak acorns). Spend a few days before your hunt glassing open areas from your truck so as to not disturb the natural patterns of the deer. If you can't be there or for smaller openings, set out a trail cam with a time-lapse trigger, such as the Moultrie Game Spy M-100 or Bushnell X-8. Photos snapped at regular intervals (say every five minutes during daylight) don't need a deer to be close enough to trigger a motion sensor and will let you know when and where deer enter a field even at a distance. Wait until the wind is right, make sure the sun is at your back, and hang and hunt a stand where the biggest buck prefers to make his grand entrance each afternoon. Note when the first deer enter the field and be settled at least an hour earlier.

3. BE A NOSY NEIGHBOR

Whether you hunt your own property or share leased land with friends or a club (or even hunt public land), hunter pressure builds as the rut and gun season approach. While it's easy to track the influx of hunters on your own land, it's just as important to get to know the people who hunt surrounding properties as well. Find out how often and when exactly they tend to hunt. Do any of them bow hunt? If not, deer that roam both properties will be less spooky. If a lot of them bow hunt, then play that to your advantage knowing that, if they mostly hunt every Saturday, you can count on them pushing deer your way. Be in the woods first and set up along likely escape routes such as a gap in a fence or the closest patch of woods if the boundary is open meadow or field. Study satellite images of neighboring properties to determine how hunters access the land and anticipate how deer will react to that pressure.

4. FEEL THE PINCH

As deer movement picks up, bucks will travel routes where they feel safe, which means sticking to the edge of cover or crossing the open from point of woods to point of woods on a field or clearcut. Like humans, they also prefer unimpeded travel routes, meaning gaps in fences, around points or bends in creeks, along the bottom edge of a bluff, or old abandoned roadways. These will also force deer to a predetermined spot. Look for these locations to heat up the last two weeks of October as pre-rut activity puts more deer seeking and chasing and really light up with the crisp arrival of November. Look for areas and natural formations that will funnel deer within a short bowshot that are also laced with well-worn trails and an abundance of scrapes and rubs. Most serious hunters that I've interviewed over the years abandon virtually every other stand location at this time of the rut phase to focus solely on pinch points.

5. ROLE CALL

If there is ever a time to use calls, now is it. Bucks are as aggressive as they're going to get, so they can be challenged with grunts and snort-wheezes and attracted by rattling. A lot of guys believe blind grunting is a waste of time. Maybe so. Do it anyway, especially if you hear a deer walking but still can't see it. Hit the grunt tube with a few deep grunts or even short-noted tending grunts every 10 or 15 minutes. It might be enough to catch a passing deer's attention that you weren't even aware was there. Even better, work the rattling horns. If both of those fail to bring a buck in that you've spotted, hit it with a snort-wheeze. A dominant buck will be hard-pressed to ignore the challenge.

6. CHOOSE SCENTS WISELY

As eager as a hunter might be to pop the cap on his premium doe estrous scent in the hopes of making a buck think a doe has come in early, he's basically, well, pissing it away. Instead, Code Blue's Mike Mattly suggests sticking with regular doe urine and buck urine for now. Bucks are challenging each other and checking scrapes often, so intruder buck urine placed in a scrape, when combined with rattling, can prove to be a deadly combination. Doe urine is good because it puts deer at ease. It makes them think other deer have just been there so the area is safe, and a deer at ease is an easier deer to arrow.

7. LIGHT IT UP WITH A SMOKEPOLE

If your state has a special muzzleloader season between archery season and gun season and you're not hunting it, it's time to start. Most blackpowder seasons are set as the pre-rut is about to transition to the rut, which makes it without doubt the best time to be in the woods. And a muzzleloader's range and accuracy will put a buck in your truck that you could only watch while using a bow.

8. THANK A LOGGER

Few things look more hellish than a lush stand of deer woods leveled by a crew of loggers. And while the loss of longstanding hardwoods can be tough to stomach, give these areas two years to grow and you'll have one of the best deer hunting spots imaginable. The sudden infusion of sunlight generates an abundance of natural browse. The new cover will be low and thick, providing enough cover for deer to bed in and feel safe on the go, but not so much that a hunter can't easily spot them. A ground blind works fine the first couple of years if no suitable trees are available for a stand, but after the third year you'll need to get high, so seek out trees on the edge or put up tower stands. The best spots are along the edge where either mature woods or a grown up former cut borders the newly opened land. Deer will work these edges both morning and evening; the does feeding, the bucks looking for does. Like a field, watch the cutover for a day or two to identify where deer bed or enter the clearcut. Before the rut kicks in, they'll move through reliable spots each day, which will help you determine where to set up. As the rut heats up, use a decoy and rattle to draw a wallhanger into range. The short cover offers the perfect mix of visibility and cover for a hunter.

9. BRING ALONG A WARDROBE CHANGE

It can still be warm at this time of the season, and nothing can compromise a hunter's scent-minimizing efforts quicker than soaking hunting clothes with sweat. To avoid this, always tote jackets or extra layers tucked in a backpack—scent-proof preferred. Never wear them while walking. To minimize getting overheated and extra sweaty, leave early so you can walk slowly to your stand, keeping your breathing and heart rate, and ultimately sweat, down. If it's really warm, wear just a single layer of breathable clothes and either on stand or just before getting there put the rest of your hunting clothes on. I've even swapped out shirts once I got to my stand, tucking the wet, dirty one into a small scent-safe or resealable plastic bag and then placing it in a pack. Wear a different set of clothing each hunt so as not to build up odor in the garments or wash them between each hunt if possible. Always use scent-free laundry detergent and dryer sheets. Another important point to remember is avoid wearing hunt clothes in camp. The

REAL ANTLERS

Pros: Low cost—just pull from a buck you've already shot; some argue more realistic, deeper tone; can use to rake leaves and limbs.

Cons: Larger; harder to pack or carry; requires two hands and more movement to use; can jab yourself with tines.

Cool Trick: Drill holes in the bases of the antlers and run a bungee cord or adjustable strap through them. You can strap them to your side or on a pack for easier toting.

RATTLE BAG

Pros: Compact; easy to pack; some models sound like the real thing; can be used with one hand.

Cons: Can't use to rake limbs or leaves; cheaper models may not sound as good or produce the volume of real antlers.

Cool Trick: Hang the bag in front of you from your stand or a limb and as a buck approaches, continue to rattle softly with one hand and the other hand at the ready on your bow or gun to seal the deal.

cooking and human smells are too numerous to combat. Remove clothes as soon as you get back from the woods, hanging them outside to remain fresh.

10. TIME YOUR HUNT

It only takes one good hunt to define a season as successful, and for the hunter willing to do his homework, a well-timed hunt can pay big dividends. After all, for a true trophy, a hunter often only gets one chance, which means hitting him when conditions are right. If a hunter has identified where a bruiser is likely bedding by catching the beast on trail cams or spotting him in action and identifying his travel routes between bedding and feeding areas as evidenced from rubs and scrapes, he can pull this one off. The window of opportunity will typically fall in the last week to week and a half of October and the first days of November, depending on where you live. You want to catch the bucks immediately before they begin really chasing. Find a day where the wind is right, the humidity low, the temperature preferably dropping with a waxing gibbous moon rising in the afternoon, and slip as close as you dare to the bruiser's bedding area using either a climber or hanging stand with sticks (whatever you can hang without making noise) three hours before the end of shooting light. Sit silently and wait. If you don't see the deer you want, in the final hour of light hit the rattling horns about every 20 minutes. If you've set up near where your identified monster lives, he should be ready to prowl and come running to your calls. Ⓗ

UTILIZING TRAIL CAM TECHNOLOGY TO LOCATE YOUR NEXT HIGH-COUNTRY MULE DEER

SEEING IS BELIEVING

WORDS & IMAGES by

MIKE QUINN

It's now crystal clear why I should have heeded the advice on the website (trailcampro.com) and purchased a metal security case to go along with my first trail camera. Hindsight is always 20/20, and, besides, I was too clueless and cheap. It takes a lowlife to steal a camera, and they typically aren't willing to backpack hours into the wilderness. My line of thinking was partially correct, as two-legged predators didn't cause the damage to my camera—a four-legged ruffian did. Admittedly, it did hold up remarkably well considering all the chewing and batting it endured, but a plastic box is not designed for a game of wilderness tetherball with a bruin. My wife's thrift and my good intention to save a few pennies paved the way for the bear to molest and destroy that fine unit. Bears 1, wife 0. Learn from my mistake and always secure your trail cameras in metal security cases. The single most important facet in killing a mule deer is scouting for them. Scouting takes time. That said, I have probably spent more disposable income and wasted more "quality time" away from family and friends scouting and hunting mule deer than any one man has the right to in several lifetimes. My wife would emphatically agree, since she and the colossus aerospace company she works for have funded most of my scouting and hunting gear purchases. (Not surprisingly, she's fond of reminding me of this fiduciary tidbit.) But one such product that has exponentially increased my ability to locate and kill trophy mulies is what my wife refers to as the "damn trail camera."

CHANGING TACTICS

Scouting the Western wilderness for mule deer is like scouting elsewhere. Most modern firearms hunters like to get up high above treeline and hike along open ridges and through sparsely timbered basins where they can glass expansive, sub-alpine mulie terrain. But today, and certainly in the future, with increased hunting pressure mounting, mulies are abandoning their traditional habitat and are adapting to life in the brush and timber.

See for yourself. Just one day into the high-country rifle opener, those sub- alpine basins once favored by summer mulies are nearly devoid of deer life. Sure, every now and then you still see deer—does, fawns, and young bucks—out in the open after first light and before last, but think about the last time you saw a 170+ class buck at dawn or dusk out in the open. Been a while hasn't it? This is simply the result of human intrusion and hunting pressure. Once-effective spot and stalk hunting tactics simply devolve into excellent exercise fraught with frustration. Self-doubt sets in, and you begin to wonder where that giant mule deer buck you spotted in mid-July or August went. What to do now? Hunt lower down the mountain, in the timber and brush, where your game cameras have already revealed to you that's where those bucks are now living!

Once I discovered what these magical devices were capable of, it dawned on me that I could finally save time—a valuable commodity in anyone's portfolio—and, more importantly, efficiently scout for bucks living in the high-country haunts I frequent. What I discovered is revealing in terms of mulie behavior and also fascinating, as I am able to review thousands of interesting photos of big-game data. I haven't been disappointed with my investment, and you won't be disappointed, either, if you follow some basic tips and techniques to maximize the trail camera's benefits and your time afield.

It's that simple. No, I didn't say easy. You will certainly sweat and suffer before it's all said and done and have a mule deer killed, gutted, and boned out, much less packed off the mountain. Still, this is exactly the strategy I began utilizing a few years ago, and it has led me to some really fine digital images of bear, mountain lion, and trophy-class mulie bucks, not to mention some outstanding trophy bucks killed in the vicinity of those cameras. Scouting this way works because it's an unobtrusive and non-threatening way to know if bucks are frequenting a favorite hunting area or not. Sure, it takes a season to master the craft and requires one to hump cameras into a few remote basins and ridges, but in my experience nothing rewarding is ever easy. Furthermore, you need to realize that the adapting mountain mulie is living in heavy forest and brush pockets as a coping mechanism to adapt and survive in a world with more hunters and predators like the wolf and mountain lion. As I write this article, though, I remain enthusiastic and encouraged by the recent trail cam images I've brought home. They have revealed to me much about the secretive behavior of the timber-living mule deer.

HOMEWORK

First, much like handloading ammunition, you need to set aside some of your "quality time" to re-evaluate your hunting area—better yet, areas—that you wish to scout using a trail cam. Even with good numbers of deer in your unit, you need to be familiar enough with your area to pick a good site for collecting digital data on any super-bucks that may be using it. Next, with your topographic map handy or simply using Google Earth, find one or several of your favorite hunting spots in the mountains. I personally have over a dozen or so hunting areas spread across Washington State where I use trail cameras. The point here is to think about alternative sites to monitor deer activity. Besides, you need to have a backup spot to hunt as a contingency should your primary area be disturbed by other hunters or suffer a natural catastrophe like a forest fire, beetle infestation, or, God forbid, a plague of bears.

One or two cameras may seem appropriate for placement at your favorite high-country hunting spot. That's fine. However, if you want to increase your knowledge concerning the numbers and behavioral activities of mule deer bucks, more is better. Yet more is only better if you can handle the logistics of multiple camera site placements and the related maintenance that goes along with them, such as swapping memory cards and replacing worn batteries every few months. I alternate six cameras between the dozen or so

slightly below the normal tree line where your hunting area is located. This is an opportune moment to locate and mark on your map the burns, blowdowns, passes between basins, avalanche chutes, and brush pockets as well as the open faces in and around your hunting area. These are the kinds of places within or just on the edge of your area hidey-holes that I'm aware of in the wilderness areas I frequent.

GETTING STARTED

The process begins in late spring and early summer or as soon as you can backpack into the high-country haunts you're familiar with. Start by placing cameras in the timber where you know or suspect mulies travel. Also place them near avalanche chutes and adjacent to brush thickets that adjoin the timber. Timber adjacent to or adjoining those open basins and ridges that you once observed bucks are another ideal place to use a camera, especially since mulies will move into that cover to bed for the day and rest after feeding in the basins at night.

The next step is to home in on the nearest timbered ridge at or

Use only lithium batteries. While more expensive initially, they last longer and are actually cheaper to use in the long run.

to concentrate placing your cameras. Why? Because those eye-popping monster bucks are somewhere nearby, and they're going to walk right past your camera and trigger a series of images on it faster than you can pronounce *Odocoileus hemionus*. Once that buck triggers the sensor, you're going to be astounded by what the camera reveals to you about your hunting area and what you've been missing in terms of the number and quality of bucks it holds. Some of the images you capture will be of bucks you only thought existed. Let me tell it to you straight: That "damn" camera is going to show you those monster bucks are there and probably always have been!

PLACEMENT

You need to give some consideration to the setup of your camera at each site you have chosen. These are places you have scouted for sign and feel are likely to capture a buck either returning to its bed or headed out to feed, or it might just be a place a buck might walk past on his way to some social interaction with other deer. Remember the name of those cameras? It starts with the word trail. So find those deer trails! Don't worry about discerning whether does, fawns, or old mossy horns himself is making the tracks or what time of day they are passing by, as you will find out soon enough with the courtesy of a time stamp embedded on the digital images you capture.

How the unit is mounted at the site you have chosen is critical. Also crucial is the removal of any offending limbs, brush, or plants in the camera's sensor detection zone. Furthermore, the effect that lighting has on your camera, its sensor, and the resultant images you capture cannot be overstated. Try to set your unit facing north or in as northerly a direction as you can to avoid sun-flare and erroneously triggering the camera's heat-in-motion sensor (PIR sensor). Often a "false positive" will occur when the camera's sensor is fooled by temperature differences in its surroundings. This mostly occurs due to the relationship the camera has with the sun lighting the area. Keep it simple at first. Point the unit in a northerly direction. You'll be pleased with the high-quality digital images it takes.

Eventually, you must find a straight and sturdy tree to mount your trail camera to. At the risk of repeating myself, mount the unit facing north! About waist high in height works well. Then lag bolt or cable lock the camera and security box to the tree. Recall, if you will, that wilderness mulie country is usually, if not always, the abode of bruins, too. Learn from others' mistakes (mine) and protect your investment from bears. Use a metal security box like I do now with all of my trail cameras.

LURE 'EM IN

Later, once your camera is mounted, that monster-racked buck is going to come right by your camera trap and trigger an image or images, and here's why: You're going to stream a copious amount of your urine 12 to 15 feet directly in front of your camera's location. Mule deer crave salt; they care not a wit about how they get it. Scrape the now-wet spot around with the toe of your boot and later on watch what happens. Well, you'll really watch your computer screen, a digital camera, or an image reader, but the images you capture will show deer and other critters licking the ground to get at the salts your urine contained. While most whitetail hunters will be appalled at this advice, mule deer won't be chased away by your infrequent application of urine. In fact, they will be drawn to it.

These camera units allow hunters to scout the territory trophy bucks inhabit in a way never before possible: remotely! Later, after analysis and much thought, we can make an informed opinion about hunting areas the cameras have determined are worthy of our time and effort. Step aside whitetail junkies; you no longer own the patent for use of these technological wonders. Trail cams work astonishingly well for Western mulie addicts, too, and I consider them at the top of my gear list along with my climbing boots and a good down sleeping bag. Ⓗ

TWEAK HIS
NOSE

MAP THE WIND ON YOUR LAND TO BEAT YOUR BUCK'S BEST LINE OF DEFENSE

 DARREN WARNER

Some of the best days to hunt are those when the barometer is falling ahead of bad weather. On these days, look for bucks in lower-lying areas, where the wind is less of a factor.

Consistently successful hunters pay attention to how the wind moves over their property, carrying with it the unmistakable stench of human odor. Doing this requires more than getting the daily weather forecast and periodically checking the wind by releasing a puff of powder in the air. Like water moving across the Earth, air currents drop over hills, shoot rapidly through narrow draws, swirl along heavy timber lines, and ricochet off steep ridge faces.

A wind map will help you better understand how air currents flow over your land. I'll explain how to create one and how to correctly use it to improve your hunting success. But before making a map, you need to understand how weather patterns affect wind movements, how deer use the wind, and how to beat a buck's sensitive nose.

HOW WIND WORKS

Wind is created when air moves from a high-pressure system to a low-pressure system. A high-pressure system is an area where the atmospheric (or barometric) pressure is greater than the pressure of the surrounding area. A low-pressure system occurs when the barometric pressure is lower than the pressure of the surrounding area.

"The prevailing wind across the U.S. is from the southwest, so the wind usually has a southerly component," said Jim Keeney, a meteorologist with the National Weather Service (NWS) Central Region Headquarters. "It's when the prevailing wind collides with a high- or low-pressure system that the wind's direction changes."

Pressure systems travel from west to east across the country. The stronger the pressure system, the greater the wind's speed. In general, high-pressure systems bring mild weather conditions, while low-pressure systems cause rain, sleet, and other "bad" weather. In a high-pressure system, wind moves in a clockwise direction around the system; wind around a low-pressure system moves counterclockwise. Note that "high" and "low" are relative terms.

"The average barometric pressure is 29.92," said John Kowaleski, another NWS meteorologist. "If you're in the 30s, you've got high pressure. Low pressure would be about 29.60."

Low-pressure systems can produce cold or warm fronts that alter the wind's direction. A fast-moving front can wreak havoc on wind direction, causing it to change several times.

WATER'S EFFECT

Large bodies of water can also make the wind switch direction. When the water temperature is at least 15 degrees Fahrenheit warmer than the air temperature, it can change the wind direction near a lake. So, if you hunt by a lake, don't be surprised if the wind blows from a different direction than the weather report said.

Terrain features, like hills, mountains and rock formations, further influence the direction wind travels. When a steady southwest wind hits the north side of a hill, the wind will wrap around the hill and switch to the east. But if you're hunting on the top of the hill, a strong wind will likely blow your scent over the top of the valley below, preventing deer from winding you and spooking.

Deer hunters know falling barometric pressure gets deer up and moving. John Jeanneney, a professional blood tracker and author of *Dead On!*, has also learned that a sudden drop in barometric pressure affects how well animals detect odors.

"All of a sudden good dogs can't smell anything," remarked Jeanneney (born-to-track.com). "We know deer can smell better than dogs, but I suspect that when the barometric pressure drops, deer can't smell as well, either."

Be in the woods when the barometer drops. Hunt small swamps, thick cover, and other safety spots whitetails use to wait out bad weather. The trick is to get there before the deer do. These areas are typically found in lower elevations, which reduce the effects of the front on wind direction.

MAKE A WIND MAP

Tricky topography, like draws, saddles, and valleys, makes the wind do funky things. Until you understand how the wind behaves in these features, hunt high and/or flat ground.

Take the guesswork out of your hunting equation by designing a wind map of your property, says writer Scott Bestul. Start by getting an aerial photo of your land. You can also use a topographic map, but it can look intimidating if you don't know how to read it. Since we know factors, such as tree foliage, air temperature, and prevailing winds, impact wind direction, create your wind map when weather conditions mimic hunting conditions.

Mark the locations of your stands on your aerial. Wait for a day with a steady wind (5-15 mph) and head to your hunting area. Go to each stand

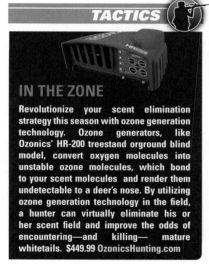

IN THE ZONE

Revolutionize your scent elimination strategy this season with ozone generation technology. Ozone generators, like Ozonics' HR-200 treestand orground blind model, convert oxygen molecules into unstable ozone molecules, which bond to your scent molecules and render them undetectable to a deer's nose. By utilizing ozone generation technology in the field, a hunter can virtually eliminate his or her scent field and improve the odds of encountering—and killing— mature whitetails. $449.99 OzonicsHunting.com

site and take a reading. Use a product like Wind Floaters, a toy bubble gun, or smoke bombs to see what the wind's doing 100-200 yards from your stand. Write down the direction the wind is supposed to be blowing from, draw an arrow showing its actual direction and note which wind directions allow you to hunt there.

Next, move to potential stand sites and record the same information. You can even map your entire hunting area.

"I start by visiting Valley 'X' on my property, and then I move to Ridgetop 'Y,' " explained Bestul. "You can even take readings on separate days, because a light wind may be blowing differently from days with strong winds."

Designing a wind map will enable you to identify two or three main air streams moving through your property and pinpoint interference areas that change the wind's direction.

"You want to insert yourself on the edge of air funnels, because deer will cruise in and out of them as they move upwind," explains wildlife consultant Neil Dougherty of North Country Whitetails (northcountrywhitetails.com).

Dougherty takes extensive wind readings by gridding each property map and ▶

25

The percentage of additional scent-collecting tissue a deer's nose contains versus a human's.

1,000

The range in yards of a whitetail's scent capability across open fields in a steady wind.

50,000

The number of scent-receptor cells per square millimeter of a whitetail deer's nose.

HIS NOSE VERSUS YOURS

Despite all that's known about whitetail deer, how well they smell remains somewhat of a mystery. We can only estimate how much better than humans deer can detect scent, but this rough equation will give you a good idea.

▶ **Surface Area:** A human has three or four square inches of scent-gathering tissue, which pales in comparison to a whitetail.

"A typical adult deer's nose is made up of more than 100 square inches of sensitive scenting tissue," said whitetail guru Tom Carpenter. "It's folded and wrinkled, as opposed to flat like ours, to increase its surface area, which helps a deer grab the faintest trace of scent."

▶ **Scent Tissue:** Since deer have about 25 times more scent-collecting tissue than humans, it's not a stretch to say they can smell 25 times better. But that's not all.

▶ **Scent Receptors:** Deer have about 50,000 scent-receptor cells per square millimeter, which is at least four times more than humans.

▶ **Add Them Up:** So whitetails have 25 times more surface area and four times more scent-receptor cells. Multiplying the two together suggests deer can smell 100 times better than humans, which is probably a conservative estimate. This means that in a steady wind blowing across open fields, what you can smell at 10 yards, deer can detect at 1,000 yards.

▶ **Adjust for Anatomy:** This doesn't take into account the fact that much more of a deer's brain is devoted exclusively to detecting and deciphering scent. We can conservatively estimate that five times more of a deer's brain is devoted solely to scent.

▶ **The Result:** Deer can probably smell 500 times better than humans.

HUNTINGTHERMALS

...nters know that thermals rise in the morn-...and fall in the evening, but many don't ...ow how deer use thermals to their advan-...e. For example, have you ever walked ...ugh a low area in the evening and run ...o a cool pocket of air? That cold pocket's ...rain area where cold air is collecting — ...d bringing all the scent in the area with it.

...W THEY WORK "As cool temperatures ...in the evening, they carry scent down

into low areas," says wildlife consultant Neil Dougherty. "These areas become sinks, collecting all the scent that was above. A savvy deer drops into those cold areas to smell everything in the area."

WHAT TO DO To prevent bucks from winding you, get to your stand no more than two hours before dark. This way, your scent will not have time to pool and cover the area before prime hunting hours. — Darren Warner

THE RIGHT STUFF

For more gear visit: nawplus.com/gear

THERMACELL HEATED INSOLES

A handheld, wireless remote control in ThermaCELL's new heated insoles allows you to select from three levels of heat emanating from the boot liners, so you can decide whether your feet need to heat up or cool down. Unlike chemical heating pads, ThermaCELL's insoles are fully rechargeable.
$129.99; ThermaCELL.com

HEATER BODY SUIT

Nothing can bring a hunt to a halt faster than cold temperatures. The Heater Body Suit provides a windproof, waterproof suit that insulates against late-season temperatures. Super-quiet and comfortable, the Heater Body Suit weighs 6–7 pounds.
$339.95–349.95; HeaterBodySuit.com

HUNTER SAFETY SYSTEM HYBRID

For the hunter who wants to maximize safety in the stand without sacrificing mobility, Hunter Safety System's new Hybrid harness is the solution. This vest system weighs 3 pounds, so hunters won't notice that they are wearing it, but it has many features found on heavier vests, including six pockets and a built-in binocular strap. Like all Hunter Safety System harnesses, the Hybrid features quiet buckles that are easy to use and snap shut in a split second.
$139.95; HunterSafetySystem.com

REMINGTON MTN. RIFLE

Entering its 25th year of production, Remington's latest rendition of the acclaimed Mountain Rifle may be their best version yet. Featuring stainless-steel construction, a feathery yet stiff Bell & Carlson aramid-fiber reinforced stock, 22-inch "mountain" contour barrel, and an X-Mark Pro trigger, this rifle packs hefty performance into a lightweight package. Available in six game-stomping cartridges. **$1,123.47; Remington.com**

SCENT-LOK FULL SEASON RECON

Scent-Lok's Full Season Recon line combines the best attributes of fleece insulation with a windproof lining. The Full Season Recon comes with a sherpa-fleece lining and weather-resistant shoulder panels that will keep hunters on-stand facing the elements with more comfort during colder-weather situations.
$179.99; ScentLok.com

REMINGTON PREMIER ACCUTIP BONDED SABOT SLUG

For whitetail hunters in states where the shotgun is your go-to firearm for tagging trophy bucks, Remington has just raised the bar. The Premier AccuTip Bonded Sabot Slug offers a level of accuracy and performance that will extend your range and dramatically improve your confidence. Steered with the Power Port Tip, the 58-caliber slug retains 95 percent of its weight and produces controlled expansion from 5 to 200 yards. Available in 2¾- and 3-inch, 12-gauge and 20-gauge versions. **$13.99–$15.99; Remington.com**

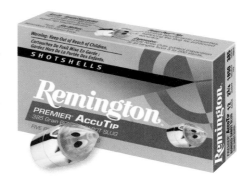

HUNT THE WIND

BY GORDON WHITTINGTON

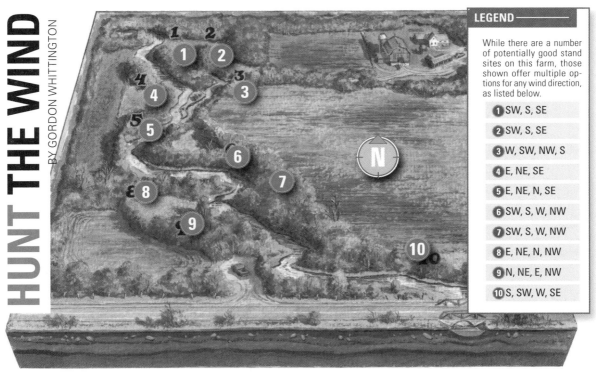

LEGEND

While there are a number of potentially good stand sites on this farm, those shown offer multiple options for any wind direction, as listed below.

1. SW, S, SE
2. SW, S, SE
3. W, SW, NW, S
4. E, NE, SE
5. E, NE, N, SE
6. SW, S, W, NW
7. SW, S, W, NW
8. E, NE, N, NW
9. N, NE, E, NW
10. S, SW, W, SE

WIND & YOUR LAND

When seeking acreage to buy, lease, or even just hunt, look for a tract well suited to the prevailing winds of autumn and winter. Many landowners wish they had.

The Ideal Setup: While no tract has perfect wind conditions at all times, this illustration shows an ideal property that provides solid hunting options in any wind. We're assuming most local fall/winter winds will have a westerly component: any direction from just west of due south on around to just west of due north. (Such winds prevail in most places, due to the earth's rotation.)

Perfect Placements: Position most of your setups to work with prevailing winds and minimize stand burnout. Here, hunting almost any westerly wind would mean parking in the farm's northeast corner and moving west or southwest to a chosen stand east of the creek.

Backup Stands: For rare easterly winds there are four setups on the creek's west side; all reachable from the parking spot near the south border. On no wind are you forced to be upwind of the most likely deer-holding cover.

For more information on land management and food plots, visit: nawplus.com/yourland

TWEAK HIS **NOSE** *continued*

checking the wind every 100 yards. Some turbulent winds make it nearly impossible to determine what the wind will do, which doesn't really worry Dougherty.

"Like hunters, mature bucks hate unpredictable winds," he said. "They make it harder for bucks to check the wind, so they often stay out of those air-funnel areas."

After you put in the time and effort to create a wind map, always let it dictate your stand selection for each hunt.

"The biggest mistake hunters make is not staying out of their best hunting stand because the wind's not right for it," said Brad Herndon, author of *Mapping Trophy Bucks.*

You can even make scent contamination work in your favor. Dougherty sets up two or three stands 150 yards apart and downwind of each other in a relatively straight line. As the season progresses and one stand site gets contaminated, he moves downwind to the next stand.

If all of this sounds like too much work, then ask yourself how many times you've missed out on taking a buck because you didn't know the wind was working against you. If your answer is anything other than "zero," then you owe it to yourself to create a wind map and update it regularly.

Along with your lucky hunting socks and your dad's .30-06, it will become something you hand down to the next generation of hunters. ⑪

TAG OUT NOW!

Follow These Tips For Late-Season Success

— BOB HUMPHREY

ONE DEFINITION OF INSANITY is repeating the same action and expecting a different outcome. Hunters are often guilty of this by hunting the same stands unsuccessfully and expecting that sooner or later the right deer will come by. Stop the insanity. It's late season — time to try a different tack and look at the property you hunt from a broader perspective. Eliminate the negative areas that aren't producing deer sightings and redirect your efforts toward what's left for positive results.

HUNT THE ROUGH STUFF

Studies show that most hunters travel only a short distance from access points and travel routes, such as footpaths, ATV trails, and farm roads. Whitetails aren't as smart as we sometimes give them credit for, but they quickly learn how to avoid humans and will eventually end up in areas where they have the fewest human encounters.

Now is the time to concentrate your efforts away from high-traffic areas to where the deer feel less pressured. Find the places where no one goes and you'll probably find the deer. Get out your topo maps and aerial photos and find the thickest cover, roughest terrain, and hardest-to-reach locations. That's where the deer will be.

DO A STAND SURVEY

Some research has shown that deer actually learn to avoid permanent stand sites. If you've been hunting the same site for an extended period, it might be time to give it a rest. Eliminate areas within 100 yards of existing stand sites that have been in place for more than a season. Do the same for any other hunters' stands. Now cross out this year's unproductive stands.

If you still have stands left, hunt them. This is the time to sit that stand you've been saving. Revisit old sites. Maybe you have a stand that used to produce, but you haven't hunted it in several years. There's a reason the deer were there before. Their patterns don't change all that much, and if there's been no disturbance, they may revert to their old ways again. Last but not least, don't be afraid to try a new location.

RESCOUT YOUR LAND

Time is of the essence, and nobody wants to waste a hunting day. But if you're not seeing deer, you may be

doing just that. Burn a day and do some in-season scouting. If you live up North, a skiff of fresh snow might help you find where the deer have moved. If not, look for the freshest sign or note where you bump bedded deer.

POST NEW TRAILCAMS

Trail cameras are invaluable for providing the "most recent information" on deer movements. If you're not using them, put some out. If you are, try moving them to new locations. Post a few trailcams and see which locations produce the most or best results.

Remember, nighttime deer activity won't do you much good, but it can help. Look closely at the times deer are triggering photos and their direction of travel. This information can help you predict when and where deer are traveling to and from bedding and feeding areas.

CHANGE LOCATIONS

If you're hunting food, move closer to bedding cover, and vice-versa. Pressured deer move less during daylight and will linger longer in bedding and staging areas. Hunt the latter in the afternoon and the former

PlotWatcher Pro
This camera offers unparalleled time-lapse technology to provide a virtual set of eyes in the field. Now you can see a video surveillance film of a particular food plot CRP field or travel corridor that will not only help you identify deer but also determine when they are using an area, how they are entering and exiting the area and how long they are staying. *(day6outdoors.com)* $250

in the morning. And get settled into both areas earlier to avoid bumping deer.

PUSH THE ENVELOPE

Establishing sanctuaries — areas where you never, ever set foot — is a great way to keep deer on the ground you hunt, but it also makes them inaccessible. With the season winding down, it might be time to cheat a little by hunting the very edges or even just inside of these inviolate areas. Do so sparingly, and remember, your first sit will likely produce your best odds. ⊕

FIND THE FOOD

Deer will seldom get on their feet this time of year except to breed and feed. As fall turns to winter, food becomes the prime motivator. Find it and you will find the deer.

Native Mast: Whitetail hunters often hunt the mast pattern early, then forget about it. But while many mast varieties are long gone by late season, those still available can provide needed nutrition and draw significant deer traffic. If heavy leaf litter makes it hard to see tracks, look for fresh pellets to indicate where the feeding action is.

Waste Grain: Agricultural areas can almost be too much of a good thing in the early season, when food is virtually unlimited. That all changes once the fields are harvested. Deer may abandon them for a while, but grain left behind by less efficient harvesting methods takes on added importance to deer and hunters alike in the late season.

Cutovers: In the big woods, a deer's winter diet consists largely of woody browse or twigs. Suckers and stump sprouts provide a readily available source of winter nutrition. Regenerating cutovers that may have been ignored earlier — when other food was still abundant — suddenly become deer magnets.
—*Bob Humphrey*

CABELA'S DIAMANTINA MERINO WOOL JACKET

Tightly packed fibers in Cabela's Diamantina jacket provide excellent warmth-to-weight ratios and can hold up to 30 percent of their weight in moisture without feeling damp or sacrificing heat retention. Available in Cabela's Outfitter Camo.
(cabelas.com) $200

AMERISTEP SWITCH

The Switch allows hunters to adjust the height of the ground blind from 60 to 88 inches so you can shoot standing up or sitting down. The lightweight, aluminum-framed blind comes with stakes and high-wind tie-downs and a backpack carrying case. Available in Realtree APG, Max-1, and Max-4.
(ameristep.com) $300

For more gear visit: **nawplus.com/gear**

REMINGTON MODEL 700 XCR II

The XCR II (Extreme Conditions Rifle) sports a stainless-steel barrel and receiver coated in Remington's matte black TriNyte Corrosion Control System to reduce glare and help combat wicked late-season weather. The stock features a Hogue rubber overmolding on the grip and forend and a SuperCELL recoil pad. *(remington.com)* $1,005

TRADITIONS VORTEK ULTRALIGHT LDR

The new 30-inch barreled, break-open Vortek LDR muzzleloader boasts better consistency, increased bullet velocity, and downrange accuracy, all while maintaining an overall weight of 6.8 pounds. A Premium CeraKote finish resists corrosion from blackpowder, cleaning chemicals, and late-season weather, and the Accelerator Breech Plug is removable by hand. *(traditionsfirearms.com)* $459

BUSHNELL G-FORCE 1300 ARC

Equipped with Bushnell's "ESP Turboprocessor," this compact range-finder offers both true horizontal distance from 5 to 99 yards in Bow Mode and bullet-drop/holdover in inches in Rifle Mode, with a maximum range of 1,300 yards. The unit can be operated in bow and rifle modes and is protected by a waterproof metal housing with rubber armor. *(bushnell.com)* $400

PORTABLE ELECTRIC FENCING is an easy way to limit deer access to certain portions of a food plot to make browse last all season long.

Moving the fence back to the first red line **(A)** will only allow deer to graze the first third of the food plot. In mid-season, moving the fence back to the second red line **(B)** will open up more browse to keep deer coming back.

Late in the season, you can open up the fencing to allow deer to graze the untouched area **(C)** at the far end, near stands 5 and 6.

PROVIDING ENOUGH QUALITY forage is a challenge for many whitetail managers. Even in a good crop year, when deer numbers are high and food is abundant, the pickings can be slim as hunting season winds down. But now, there's a practical solution: movable, solar-powered electric fencing that puts you in control of when deer access an area. Recent research at the Institute for White-tailed Deer Management & Research in Texas has shown just how effective these fences can be.

Similar fences have been around the livestock industry since the 1930s, but only recently have the features been adapted for use in managing deer. For a few hundred dollars you can now control several acres of forage, by deciding

For more information on land management and food plots visit: **nawplus.com/yourland**

how to configure the fence originally and then changing it as the season progresses.

Although these fences are only about waist high, few deer will jump over or try to crawl under. Thus, while the forage outside the fence might be eaten to the ground, what's inside remains pristine. It's up to you to decide when and how to adjust the fence to keep the deer coming back without burning through the total supply of forage too soon.

This illustration shows how you might open up a plot as the year progresses, ultimately leaving the whole planting accessible in late season. And there are

good stand choices for being close to the action all season long. Stands 1 and 2 are obvious options for early-season hunting, while 3 and 4 will be near the most activity in mid-season. Stands 5 and 6 overlook the area in which deer should concentrate their feeding in the late season.

QUICK TIP

CALORIES COUNT

Winter's cold increases the importance of a deer's ability to balance calories consumed with calories burned. They reduce the latter by seeking out more favorable environs.

In the big woods, deer seek the ameliorating effects of dense softwood cover, which breaks the wind and reduces snow depth.

In industrial timberland, look for deer in dense, uncut hardwood bottoms or young, regenerating pine stands.

In hilly terrain, deer will generally spend more time on south-facing slopes, which receive the greatest amount of sunlight during the day.

– Bob Humphrey

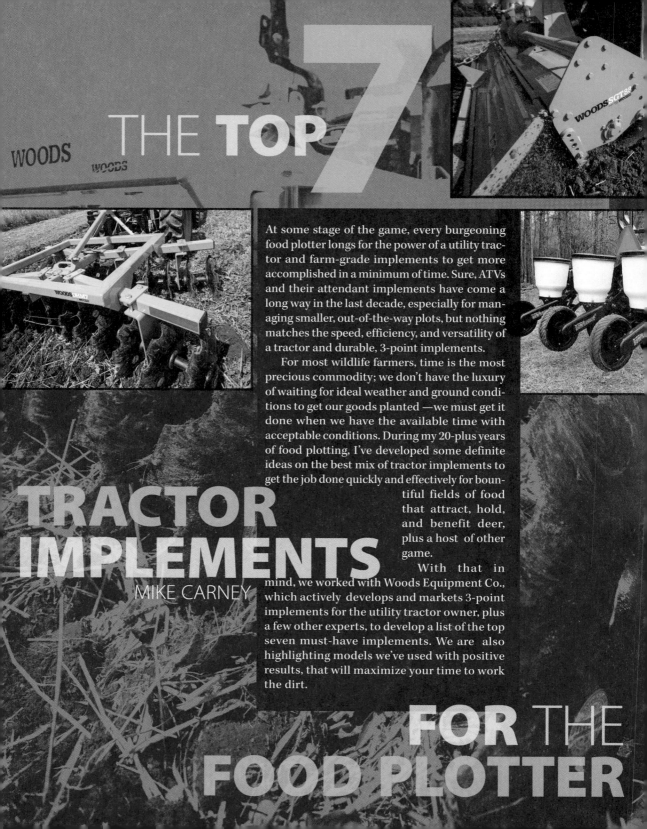

THE TOP 7

TRACTOR IMPLEMENTS

MIKE CARNEY

FOR THE FOOD PLOTTER

At some stage of the game, every burgeoning food plotter longs for the power of a utility tractor and farm-grade implements to get more accomplished in a minimum of time. Sure, ATVs and their attendant implements have come a long way in the last decade, especially for managing smaller, out-of-the-way plots, but nothing matches the speed, efficiency, and versatility of a tractor and durable, 3-point implements.

For most wildlife farmers, time is the most precious commodity; we don't have the luxury of waiting for ideal weather and ground conditions to get our goods planted —we must get it done when we have the available time with acceptable conditions. During my 20-plus years of food plotting, I've developed some definite ideas on the best mix of tractor implements to get the job done quickly and effectively for bountiful fields of food that attract, hold, and benefit deer, plus a host of other game.

With that in mind, we worked with Woods Equipment Co., which actively develops and markets 3-point implements for the utility tractor owner, plus a few other experts, to develop a list of the top seven must-have implements. We are also highlighting models we've used with positive results, that will maximize your time to work the dirt.

from left: TILLER • CULTIPACKER • MOWER   Bottom from left: DISC HARROW • PLANTER • SEEDER • SPRAYER

ROTARY MOWER

A rotary mower is an invaluable management tool. Uses include clearing fields of heavy grass, brush, and second growth; cutting up a previous season's crop residue, like cornstalks, sunflowers, and bean vines for reincorporation to the soil; creating game trails through otherwise impenetrable cover in the woods and around stand access points; plus maintaining annual plantings like clover and alfalfa.

Woods, the originators of tractor-mounted rotary cutters and the inventors of the "Batwing" cutter, offers a variety of single-spindle models for tractors from 15 to 200 hp. A couple we have used and recommend are the Brushbull BB60X and the BB72X, in cutting widths of 60 and 72 inches respectively, for tractors from 25 to 65 hp. Both models will cut brush up to 1.5 inches in diameter and are Category 1 hitch compatible. For super-tough jobs on brush up to three inches in diameter, my personal cutter, the Woods BB720X, is a brush-eating machine, intended for tractors 30 to 120 hp.

All models have a six-year gearbox warranty and feature quick-change blade pins, stump jumper protection, two-inch tubular rear bumpers for backing over brush, a full frame design with 3x4-inch structural internal tubes that reinforce all stress points, and smooth slope top decks to shed material and moisture. These are ultra-tough cutters that will likely outlast your tractor.

SPRAYER

Whether it's to burn down a field before planting or to kill weed competition growing in your plots, you'll need a quality sprayer you can easily calibrate for precise chemical applications such as Roundup. I recommend large-capacity models over 50 gallons so that once you are set up and calibrated, you're not heading back to the barn to mix and refill the tank after every acre of spraying. A longer spray boom will minimize total passes required to cover a field; look for at least 10-feet of coverage.

Fimco is synonymous with sprayers, and they're widely available at outlets such as Tractor Supply. I've used a variety of their ATV and 3-point models, and they're easy to calibrate and adjust. If you have a lot

PLANTINGS

I am often asked what I think is the single best warm-season planting for deer. Without doubt, if I could only plant one warm-season wildlife food in the Midwest, it would be soybeans. Beans provide succulent, leafy forage for deer to eat during the summer, and if deer densities aren't too high and/or you protect young plants with electric fencing, like those from Gallagher (gallagherusa.com) as well as Battenfeld Technologies (battenfeldtechnologies.com), you will have some residual grain left into the winter months—if you have a minimum of three to five acres for a small plot.

The best two seed varieties I've tried are Real World Wildlife Seed (realworldwildlifeseed.com) and Eagle Seed's (eagleseed.com) Wildlife Manager's Mix. Both varieties are Round-up Ready but have slightly different characteristics. For maximum leafy yield and summer browse, the Eagle soybean varieties are unmatched. For maximum bean production while still yielding good summer leaf tonnage, go with Real World, which has a bean pod that is shatter resistant and will hold beans in the pod all winter long. We planted half-acre plots of these two varieties side-by-side, and, just advertised, Eagle was the preferred brand for summer forage, while the Real World produced more and larger seeds that the deer readily consumed by early December. We plant Eagle seeds where we want summer foraging to occur and the Real World variety where we want to kill deer come hunting season.

of smaller plots in hard-to-reach areas, their 25-gallon ATV-25-71 is a good choice, but you will be refilling/remixing after every acre of treatment. The LG-60-3PT is the top choice for tractor-mounted models, holding 60 gallons with a fold-up, breakaway, 140-inch boom for covering a wide swath of rows. You will also need at least a 6-roller pump to attach to your PTO, and some of the

best are from Hypro (hypropumps.com); look at the 7560XL pump with stainless components for maximum corrosion protection against chemicals like glyphosate.

DISC HARROW

A disc harrow is a vital tool for breaking new ground, incorporating old crop residue, and final prepping of the ground before planting large seed. But there are huge differences in quality and performance with many of the smaller 3-point models available. First, match the hp of your

tractor to the hp rating the disc requires. I recommend the heaviest disc your tractor can pull for maximum groundbreaking ability. I also prefer dual-disc gangs that are indepen- dently adjustable for angle, and I like notched blades up front followed by smooth, finishing-type blades in the rear. This arrangement allows for the most versatile setup options to meet the conditions of the soil, whether that's maximum tillage or finishing passes just prior to planting.

A model that I've come to love for its incredible versatility is the Woods seven-foot DHM7, for tractors 36 to 70 hp. (If your tractor is lower hp, look at the DHM5 or DHM6 for tractors down to 28 hp.) The DHM7 weighs a full 900 pounds and features independently adjustable gangs at 0, 7, 14, and 21 degrees, conveniently set with drop-in locking pins, no tools required. The triple-sealed, self-aligning disc bearings assure long life, and the hefty 3x3-inch structural tubular construction makes this disc a tough, reliable performer for any tillage job.

TILLER

For lighter ground that's been worked or previously planted, a tiller is one of the best tools for creating a fine seedbed—often in just one pass—and it chops and incorporates field residue better than any other implement. If you are planting any fine seed—like clover, alfalfa, warm season grasses, or small cereal grains—a tiller is invaluable for creating the optimal seedbed, and depending on soil conditions, I often use one even when planting beans and corn. Tillers can be had in forward or reverse rotation. On initial pass, reverse rotation will often till deeper and faster than forward rotation, and it creates a finer layer of soil.

The only reverse rotation tiller I've used is the Woods TCR74 for compact tractors up to 45 hp, and it works like a charm for one-pass soil preparation. For moist, wet, heavy, rocky ground, Woods SGT88 forward rotation tiller is a beast, compatible with tractors 40 to 70 hp. If you have rougher ground, this powerhouse tiller can dig in up to eight inches deep and has an extra heavy-duty transmission for the toughest tilling jobs.

A good food source will attract and, more importantly, hold deer like this seven-year-old monster the author arrowed on his property.

PLANTER

A planter is the ideal tool when sowing staples like corn, soybeans, and other larger seeds that benefit from exact populations per acre and require weed treatment during their growing cycle.

There are very few commercially available food plot planters. Many opt for used John Deere 4-row 7000 and 7100 models, but unless you know exactly what you are looking at, it's tough to evaluate condition. The only viable commercially made planter I'm aware of for food plotters is the economical Yetter 71 row planter, available from Midwest Wildlife Management (midwestwildlife.com), which is available in 2-, 3- or 4-row configurations. This time-tested workhorse has planted literally millions of rows over the years. The 71 can plant at your exact seed spacing and depth, maximizing plant populations and yield for your efforts. I've used one for three seasons, I like it's large, 1.3-bushel seed hoppers; no-tools required adjustable seed depth; adjustable down-pressure springs for planting in varied soil conditions; parallel linkages, which allow the independent planter units to flex over varying ground contours for uniform seed depth; and huge combinations of plates and drive gears for achieving nearly any plant population per acre imaginable. You will need to order specific seed plates that match your preferred seed from Lincoln Ag Products (lincolnagproducts.com). This compact planter can be shipped anywhere in the U.S. and is a fast, accurate solution for high-yield food plotting.

SEEDER

A precision seeder, while not an absolute necessity, is damn convenient and time maximizing for accurately planting small grains like clover, alfalfa, cereal grains and warm season grasses. If you food plot for long, you eventually want one to replace inaccurate, broadcast seeders, especially when you're dealing with expensive clover and alfalfa seed.

Last fall I enjoyed a sneak peak field trial of the Woods PSS84 Precision Super Seeder to put in our fall foodplots of oats, rye, wheat, and clover, and you can color me impressed. The heavy duty frame of this seeder keeps it firmly engaged to the ground for precise seed depth control, and seeding rates are accurately adjusted on the large capacity seed cups with a single lever. The standard, cool season box can be combined with two additional seed boxes, one legume seed box and one warm season/native grass seed box, to enable plating anything from radishes to soybeans, as well as prairie grasses and wild flowers. Using the optional legume seed box allows you to effectively plant two types of seed at two different depths all in one pass, saving time and fuel. All seed boxes can be engaged/disengaged with the removal of a single lynch pin. This allows you to plant exactly what you want and reduces wear on parts that aren't needed for a particular application. An optional trailing cultipacker firms the seed.

CULTIPACKER

A 3-point cultipacker is a heavy, 400 to 1000 pound, cast iron set of rollers used to firm a loose seedbed prior to planting or to create good seed-to-soil contact on broadcasted seeds. It's simple technology, but an implement you will need for top results. For speed and efficiency, look for the widest, heaviest model your tractor can accommodate to limit passes required.

I've used Omni's (omni-mfg.com) Cultipacker series in widths from 48 to 96 inches, and they give you everything you want at a very affordable price. I've also used Everything Attachments (everythingattachments.com) cultipackers with 15-inch wheels and convenient E-Z Fold Skid Stands. ⊕

MULE DEER

TWO PASSIONATE HUNTERS MAKE

JOSEPH VON BENEDIKT

WHITETAILS

A CASE FOR THEIR FAVORITE DEER

DOUG HOWLETT

Su·pe·ri·or
Higher in range, status, or quality.

I could take the low road and be really offensive by saying that all it takes to be a successful whitetail hunter is 1) property or money to lease property, 2) a treestand, 3) a zombie-like ability to sit and stare at an empty field for days on end, and 4) a rifled shotgun that will plop a slug onto a paper plate at 100 yards. I could point out that mule deer hunters must be wilderness woodsmen; must know mulie habitat, nomadic habits, and migration patterns; must be able to cover vast amounts of country in search of a bruiser buck; and—once that buck is found—must be able to pull off a difficult, cross-canyon shot in unpredictable winds.

I could point all that out, but that would be a bit harsh. No, I'll be more diplomatic and just let mule deer characteristics and traits support my argument that they are the superior big-game species.

FIGHT OR FLIGHT

Though whitetails are wired with a short fuse and an incredibly thin panic-and-scram point, mule deer are cagier. They strategically sneak away from danger and are smart enough to pause when they feel safe and turn to figure out what the danger was and how to avoid it next time. Thankfully for hunters, they often offer a fleeting but excellent shot opportunity when they turn, unlike the less courageous whitetail that keeps steaming right on out of sight.

Old-timers, back before hunters figured out

Utah-born Joseph von Benedikt grew up in the heart of big mule deer country and has hunted them for over two decades in six states. Incurably addicted to quiet desert canyons and frosty timberline ridges—and their long-eared inhabitants—his goal is to still be hunting mule deer in his 90s. Shooting a 200-class typical and a gnarly, massive non-typical buck along the way wouldn't hurt, either.

Lead·er
Something that ranks first.

When considering all of the game animals there are to hunt in North America, one animal stands head and antlers above the rest. It is this un-rivaled leader, beyond all other species, big or small, that drives the hunting industry, virtually causes some towns to shut down when opening day rolls around, and is sought after by more hunters in this country than any other species. That's right, the whitetail deer is—and always will be—king of game species in this country, and it certainly holds dominion over the other commonly hunted deer in the United States: the mule deer.

Doug Howlett was born in Virginia, for which the whitetail is scientifically named (*Odocoileus virginianus*), and grew up hunting in the Southeast where the entire region is a bedding area. Earn-A-Buck there meant you traipsed thick pine forests and lurked in mosquito-infested swamps just to kill a 128-inch buck. He now hunts across the whitetail's range and is addicted to chasing big bucks in new terrain.

Sure, the mule deer holds its rightful place among our cherished hunting traditions, and it certainly has the potential for jaw-dropping racks, with the much sought-after 30-inch-wide rack still a possibility in some select areas where mulies roam. But with challenging access, struggling populations in some areas of its already limited range, and the need to draw for tags in many places, most American hunters will never get the opportunity to pursue a mule deer and, as a result, will never really care either way.

Mule deer, with limited tag availability and their limited Western range, are an adventure species—something to hunt during a single trip, maybe even a once-in-a-lifetime trip. Whitetails, on the other hand, inspire an entire culture. They are a lifestyle species, one that hunters completely live for, scheduling their entire year around the opening week of deer season. As such, they have won the rightful distinction at the top of our list

When it comes to sheer bone, the mule deer reigns supreme. The World Record Typical mule deer was taken in 1972, in Dolores County Colorado. It scores 226⁴/₈.

how predictable whitetails were and lowered their principles enough to hunt from trees, thought mule deer stupid in comparison to their little eastern cousins. Nothing could be further from the truth. If anything, the opposite is true. Ask any broadly experienced deer hunter and you'll be told a mature mule deer is perhaps the hardest of all trophies to collect today.

PREDICTABLE

Whitetails are wretchedly predictable, allowing one to successfully ambush them while one's comfortably perched in the local white oak. Mule deer, on the other hand, are both nomadic and non-territorial, or at least their territories are vastly larger. A big buck may find a comfortable spot that provides cover, food, and what little water he needs and hunker down for a while to fatten up against the rut, but at the first slight disturbance he'll be gone for another drainage miles away. And it might be a year or more before he's seen back in the original spot.

Seasonal nomadic habits add challenge, too. You can't pick up a big shed antler and whisper with quavering voice, "Here is where I'm putting my rubberized tin treestand this fall!" No, about all that shed antler will tell you is that a big buck wintered there and is now

(cont. on p.65)

of game animals, earning a spot commensurate with the mystery, beauty, and challenge they bring to American fields and forests, from the Atlantic Ocean to the lower elevations of the Rockies, from Mexico up to Canada.

ALL ACCESS WHITETAILS

Since teetering on the brink of extinction in the early 1900s, the whitetail's comeback is without peer as one of the greatest conservation success stories in the world. Today, whitetails roam throughout much of the continental United States and portions of Canada and Mexico. They are among the most recognized animals among hunters and nonhunters alike and can be hunted within an hour's drive of nearly 80 percent of the U.S. population.

They are one of the most resilient and adaptable wildlife species as well, living in a variety of habitats, including swamps, mountains, farmland, hardwoods, plains, river bottoms, and even inside the brushy interiors of urban and suburban highway on-ramps and off-ramps. They can thrive in a pocket of cover surrounded by homes just as well as they rule the wide-open agrarian landscape of the Midwest. Sadly, the same cannot be said for the mule deer, which has actually ceded some lower elevation habitat to whitetails as they continue to adapt and expand. *(cont. on p.66)*

Nearly perfectly symmetrical, the World Record whitetail deer, taken by Milo Hanson in Biggar, Sasketchewan scores an astounding 213⁵/₈.

WHITETAIL

TALE OF THE TAPE
Just the facts ma'am, just the facts.

MULE DEER

Total population in the U.S.: 3.5 million
Total hunter harvest per year: 300,000
Highest state population: Colorado (400,000)
Highest state harvest: Colorado (33,000)
Success rate of hunters: Colorado (45%)
Number of states with mule deer: 18
Total number of mule deer hunters: 1.13 million
Highest over-the-counter tag price: $609.25 (Arizona)
World Record B&C Typical: 226⅛" (Colorado)
World Record B&C Non-Typical: 355⅜" (Alberta)
World Record P&Y Typical: 205" (Mexico)
World Record P&Y Non-Typical: 274⅞" (Colorado)
The most B&C Typical entries: 696 (Colorado)
The most B&C Non-Typical entries: 265 (Colorado)

WHITETAIL

Total population in the U.S.: 32 million
Total hunter harvest per year: 6 million
Highest state population: Texas (4 million)
Highest state harvest: Texas (546,000)
Success rate of hunters: Texas (60%)
Number of states with whitetails: 48
Total number of whitetail hunters: 10.9 million
Highest over-the-counter tag price: $551 (Iowa)
World Record B&C Typical: 213⅝" (Saskatchewan)
World Record B&C Non-Typical: 333⅞" (Missouri)
World Record P&Y Typical: 204⅘" (Illinois)
World Record P&Y Non-Typical: 294" (Ohio)
The most B&C Typical entries: 973 (Wisconsin)
The most B&C Non-Typical entries: 546 (Illinois)

Data provided by Boone and Crockett, Pope and Young, Mule Deer Foundation, and QDMA.

© Tony Campbell-fotolia.com

summering somewhere in the far blue mountains, and that if you're really, really lucky you might find his sheds next year, too, because you're not going to find and shoot him there.

CALL SHY

Calling mule deer? Forget it. With rare exceptions, mule deer are not responsive to calling or rattling. Sure, some half-deer guru may claim that he can coax mule deer within sunflower seed-spitting distance every try—and maybe he can even prove it—but as a whole, the West's long-eared deer just aren't susceptible to love-stricken bleats or the testosterone-infused clashing of plastic antlers. Mule deer aren't as vocal or vocally responsive and to my regret—yes, I'll admit it—just aren't likely to be called into shooting distance, grunting and wheezing and blowing steam like a rut-crazed whitetail buck.

Being non-territorial, mule deer bucks avoid another Achilles' heel by which a whitetail may be laid low: mulies don't consistently tend scrapes. They make them on occasion, but good luck hunting over one. Randomly wandering in search of love, a big mulie buck can't often be ambushed, even if you are lucky enough to hold a tag in one of the few areas where the rut coincides with the hunting season.

BIG COUNTRY

The very habitat that mule deer prefer indicates inherent superiority. Why live in a cornfield with a muddy, poison ivy infested ravine behind it when the timberline basins of the Rockies and the wide, quiet deserts of the West beckon? Don't get me wrong: I'm thrilled that whitetails prefer agricultural land, because whitetail encroachment on mule deer habitat is hard on the mule deer. Here, I've got to concede one to the whitetails: they are simply more adaptable and better suited for survival among the burgeoning human population. Which is another reason I prefer mule deer. I'm not real adaptable to living with humanity, either.

Much as I enjoy a foggy morning in a stand in a good patch of Midwestern timber, there's nothing quite like hunting high-elevation wilderness country. Vast, wind-swept ridges, misty canyons, and wildflower-filled alpine meadows are what mule deer call home, and I love 'em for it. It's the kind of country you feel honored to even

(cont. on p.68)

MULE DEER

With their widespread presence and big-game cache, it is no wonder more hunters—by the millions—hunt whitetails. They are easily accessed through hunt club memberships, private leases, private land ownership, outfitter services, and even on public land. Most land leased for hunting east of the continental divide is leased for the right to hunt whitetails. And, when it's time for hunting season to begin, the opening days in respective states with rich hunting traditions account for more days off from work than any other species. In fact, some small towns in such deer-rich states as West Virginia, Pennsylvania, and Ohio come to a virtual standstill as hunters take time off to enjoy the ritual of deer hunting.

It is the famed hunting camps in places like Maine, the Adirondacks of New York, the mountains of Pennsylvania, and in the Upper Peninsula of Michigan, just as much as the big hunt clubs of the South, that feed the lore of the hunter in American culture. Iconic images of family and friends gathered for a week of hunting in a big woods camp, men escaping the yoke of the time clock or office desk to escape to the wilderness where they can be...well...men, are images built around none other than the whitetail deer.

CHALLENGE AND OPPORTUNITY

Its ability to blend in virtually unseen in all manner of habitat, combined with its amazing senses of smell and hearing and an almost supernatural wariness that helps it survive, make the whitetail one of the most challenging animals to hunt, yet not so challenging that it's impossible.

Old men or kids content with seeing game and getting a shot to fill the freezer can sit a stand or stalk the forest each season with the relative confidence that at some point they will find success. Meanwhile, for the ardent big-buck devotee, patterning deer throughout the year, following a scent-control regimen that would've made the late Howard Hughes look unclean, and filling virtually every free minute to be in the woods to better understand his quarry is the price that must be paid in order to score on one of the monsters of this species. *(cont. on p.69)*

Photo Credit: Tom Martineau – The Raw Spirit

CROWNING THE KING OF DEER

Michael Waddell

Picking the best deer in this great land is a hands-down, no-contest easy choice. It is obvious to anyone who has hunted both; it's the whitetail. Or mule deer…or whitetail…. Heck, maybe it isn't so easy after all!

I cut my teeth hunting those sneaky old whitetail bucks on my family's farm in Booger Bottom, Georgia, so I hold them in high regard. And rightfully so—an old whitey anywhere you find him is

a cagey animal. To reach maturity, he has made it through several seasons, has probably had numerous encounters with hunters, and is about as jacked up as any animal in the world. You can occasionally luck into a trophy buck, but more often Mother Nature rewards the persistent and diligent. Scent control is paramount, but stand location, solid preseason scouting, and pure patience pays dividends.

If I could do nothing but hunt whitetails the rest of my life, I would die happy. At least I used to think that…then I traveled out West and fell in love with mulies.

The allure to mule deer, at least for me, is the country. The West is hands-down some of the most scenic country in the world, and if the game Monopoly had a Western version, mule deer would be living on Boardwalk. From desert scenes right out of a John Wayne movie to the highest of the Rocky Mountains, you will find majestic mule deer.

Another mark in favor of mule deer is their sheer size—they are just an impressively built animal made for bounding up shale chutes and across ridges, and when it comes to pure bone on top of their head, it is really hard to beat a big ole mule deer.

As for hunting skills—all I can say is they are just different. Both require their own unique set of skills completely different from one another. A mule deer requires a hunter to be a masterful stalker and a darn good shot (especially with a stick and string). A whitetail requires patience and paying attention to details. Both different skill sets, both enjoyable and fulfilling.

After hunting both whitetail and mule deer and killing my share of good ones, all I can say is it would be a sad day if I had to choose between them. I like them both for what they are!

occupy, let alone wander through with your favorite rifle or bow.

SIZE MATTERS

Shifting from philosophical to concrete, measureable differences, mule deer have bigger racks, and most hunters like big racks. Nutrition, age, and other general influences being roughly equal, an average mature mule deer buck will grow some 160 to 190 inches of antler, as opposed to a similar whitetail, which will grow 130 to 170 inches. Bigger—sometimes much bigger—growth occurs in both species, but in reality such occurrences are anomalies.

Western guides usually have to stress caution to first-time mulie hunters from the East because a three-year-old mule deer is as big as a gagger whitetail and frequently causes trigger fingers to twitch uncontrollably. This in turn can cause hard feelings when the three-year-old buck's granddaddy jumps up and out of his bed at the shot.

BETTER RIFLEMEN

Speaking of trigger fingers, successful mule deer hunters have to be better riflemen than whitetail hunters. Aside from some limited exceptions, actually shooting a mule deer is typically much more challenging than shooting a whitetail. Mule deer country is big, steep, and rugged. Shots across canyons and steep uphill or downhill angles are common. If you're lucky enough to get a shot at a good buck, the wind can be blowing three different directions at three different speeds between his position and yours. Rifle, optic, ammo, and shooter all have to be above par. And you've got to shoot from field positions; you don't have the steadying effect of the rubberized highchair bar of your tin treestand.

NO FENCES

Finally—and perhaps most importantly when considering the extraordinary challenge of taking a trophy mule deer— a big mulie can't really be bought. Sure, if you've got a private jet and can fork over $100,000 or more for a Governor's tag in Utah or some other top mule deer state and are willing to hire a whole bevy of professional guides to spend their summer scouting, you've got a pretty good chance at shooting a whopper come fall. But even that's not guaranteed. And though private land hunts increase your chances of success by limiting pressure from competing

Photo Credit: Vic Schendel

hunters, most of the true trophy bucks are taken from remote wilderness areas or limited-draw hunts. Don't crucify me for writing this, but monster whitetails are as available as your extra cash. If you've got the money, you can—on demand—shoot a 200-plus-inch whitetail. I know most of us like to think we wouldn't, but that's not the point. As a species, courtesy of that adaptability mentioned earlier, whitetails flourish under captivity, whereas mule deer do not.

Any time you see a big, mature mule deer buck on some lucky hunter's wall, you know he took it the hard way. And that, my friends, more than perhaps everything else, is why I respect mule deer—and dedicated mule deer hunters—more than whitetails. Ⓗ

Vic Schendel

online chatroom discussion. But Hanson's record has yet to be broken and remains the Holy Grail of hunting records, one every hunter dreams of breaking.

DRIVING AN INDUSTRY

In case the hunting challenge, available opportunity, and beauty of the whitetail deer as the icon of our nation's hunting tradition isn't enough to convince you it rules over mule deer as the top deer species in this country, here's another reason: Whitetails are an economic driver like no other species known to man!

As the most sought-after game animal in the country, whitetails are the focus of entire businesses and industries, such as scent companies, scent-free clothing companies, treestand makers, and wildlife seed distributors. Whitetails were the impetus for today's ubiquitous camouflage clothing and drive many innovations and developments within the gun and ammo industries. Without whitetails, the entire archery industry would be so small as to be rendered the exclusive domain of mom-and-pop businesses and impassioned devotees of stick and string rather than the increasing dominion of large corporate entities.

Take whitetail coverage out of outdoor television and magazines and you'd lose probably 70 percent of all the hunting programs on TV and half the pages and covers in magazines. In magazines such as this one, whitetails receive coverage in virtually every issue. Can't say the same for mule deer. Unless it's a magazine devoted to mule deer, you will be hard-pressed to find a mule deer column. But most mags have the business sense to include one devoted to whitetails.

Yep, whether examining their place in American hunting history, the challenge they provide the majority of hunters in our country, or the economic engine that is whitetail deer hunting, the whitetail is rightfully the king of all game animals and certainly rules the debate over which is better when compared to its niche cousin, the mule deer. ⏺

Big bucks become almost like ghosts, reclusive and solitary, moving mostly at night and maintaining very small home ranges when hunting pressure is at its peak. Hunters must often compete against the weather, terrain, and the pressure from other hunters as much as they work to overcome the whitetail's senses. All of this adds up to a quarry worthy of all the respect given to it by those who pursue whitetails with a passion.

THE HOLY GRAIL OF RECORDS

Few things stir the soul and inspire the hunter like the sight of a giant rack atop the head of a whitetail. Able to grow in excess of 200 combined inches with as many as a dozen or even twice that number of points, big whitetail bucks are obviously a much sought-after trophy. Few hunters could tell you who holds the record for the largest mule deer ever taken, but nearly anyone who hunts has heard the name of Milo Hanson, a Saskatchewan hunter, who has held the title for the typical World Record buck since 1993.

Since then, other bucks have challenged the Canadian giant, each one creating a buzz of media and

TURNBULL MFG. CO.
BLOOMFIELD, NY
U. S. A.

SAFE

FIRE

My Kansas deer season had a few days to run when, on a December morning, I headed down the ridge below the house and clambered up into my stand. It isn't exactly "my" stand; it's one of several, and not actually my favorite. But I had a couple of friends coming in to hunt, so I wanted to leave my favorite stands —and what I think of as the best part of my woods—for them. I guess you also couldn't say it's "my" deer

A REALLY SPECIAL DEER RIFLE

CRAIG BODDINGTON

A GORGEOUS AR DESIGNED FOR HUNTING GETS FIELD-TESTED DURING THE KANSAS DEER SEASON.

season; the regs apply to everyone equally. And if you look at it another way, my ability to use the remaining days would be limited.

It didn't really matter. This particular year I'd put a good bit of time in the woods. I'd hunted a couple of weeks during the archery season and seen some decent bucks. As usual, or at least as usual when I'm hunting my little Kansas farm, I'd let a couple of bucks walk by that I knew I should have taken ...and I'd seen a couple of better bucks that weren't quite close enough. I could say the same about the first few days of rifle season—but now I was down to the tail end, or at least my tail end, and that simplifies things a bit.

It was barely chilly that morning, not as cold as a deer hunter should hope for, but extremely pleasant to sprawl out on the Ameristep double stand while the sun climbed slowly behind me. I saw a couple of does early, and then a little 6-pointer came down the ridge in front of me. He wasn't the least bit tempting, but he was interesting in that this is the opposite direction I expect movement from this stand...and yet, in the relatively few times I've sat there, that's where about half the deer have come from.

It was getting late and warming up nicely, and I was starting to think about how much longer I should hold off going to work on a pesky deadline for a hated Editor (probably for this very magazine) when I caught a bit of movement off my right shoulder. OK, that's where the deer are supposed to come from! It was a mature doe, followed by a yearling—and then another doe. They angled across my front, and although none pulled the classic giveaway of looking back, I had a feeling that wasn't all. So I held as perfectly still as I'm capable of, rifle up across my body, weight resting on the padded rail.

My sixth sense isn't perfect—I might have been wrong a dozen times just in that season—but this time I was right... a nice buck trailed out behind the does. He was sort of a medium 8-pointer, certainly not one of the big bucks, but not one of my babies. I weighed the odds, but only briefly, and as he stepped into the clear, I raised the rifle. The shot was that rare perfect left-hand shot; the rifle was already angled in the general direction of the deer, so all I needed to do was bring the muzzle down and the butt up to my shoulder. When I did this, the crosshairs were already on the point of his shoulder as he quartered to me, so I slipped the safety to "fire" and squeezed the trigger.

A GREAT DEER LOAD

The cartridge was a .308 Winchester, the specific round a plain-Jane 150-grain softpoint from Federal blue-box Power-Shok—no premium upgrade implied and no designer brand identified as the specific bullet. It was a spitzer bullet with quite a bit of lead exposed at the nose. Since the box didn't say "Hi-Shok," Federal's long-running proprietary softpoint, I would bet that the original source of that bullet was Hornady, but it really doesn't matter. The load grouped fairly well in the rifle—much better than necessary for "minute of buck" at 60 yards.

That sharp-pointed, lead-tipped 150-grain bullet had a bullet diameter of .308-inch, what we call a ".30 caliber," so for at least a hundred years we've thought of that weight and diameter of bullet as a "deer bullet." In calibers from .30-30, .30 Remington, and .300 Savage on up to the fastest .300 magnums, millions of deer have been taken with similar bullets...by generations of hunters.

The specific case dimensions of the cartridge I fired this bullet from are designated ".308 Winchester." This cartridge and I share the same year of birth, 1952, a different time when the Korean War was dragging on, Eisenhower was elected President, and this strange new gadget called "telly-vision" was just starting to work its way into American homes. But despite our similar age, it's no secret that I have never been a huge fan of the .308 Winchester. Sorry, can't help it; I like the .30-06 better! However, I don't have to have a personal affinity for a cartridge to

respect it. The .308 Winchester offers a good 95 percent of the capability of the longer-cased .30-06 (which is not damning with faint praise at all), and since it does it from a shorter case, it can fit into more compact actions and, on average, is a more accurate cartridge than the .30-06.

While it isn't my personal top choice, it was my Dad's favorite, the cartridge he took almost all of his big game with. It's also a cartridge I have used quite a bit, and in several action types: bolt, lever, and semiautomatic. So, when this Kansas whitetail took a 150-grain lead-core expanding bullet from a .308 Winchester on the point of his left shoulder, the results weren't surprising. The bullet traversed the chest cavity diagonally and exited behind the right shoulder. The buck spun away, made maybe three steps, and was down.

NOT A BAD DEER RIFLE...

I waited for a couple of minutes, and then I cleared the rifle and lowered it on the line we keep on our stands for that purpose. While fiddling with the rope, I took a moment to admire the rifle one more time. It had just demonstrated that it was a pretty good deer rifle, but, after all, what was there to prove? We know about the .308, and we know about the 150-grain .30-caliber bullet. We even know about the 3-9X Leupold the rifle wore—I think I had it on 4X to fit the size of the clearing.

The rifle, however, was a bit of a departure for me. It was one of a first run of Doug Turnbull's TAR-10 rifles, which, in turn, are also a significant departure for Doug Turnbull. I think he's probably best-known today for his classic lever actions, but he also works with Colt

These are just a half-dozen rifles among the 90 manufacturers offering what are generally very similar products. Mechanically, the Turnbull gun is identical...but it offers a very different look!

single actions and 1911s, and he's justly famous for restoring (and upgrading) classic American firearms. If none of that rings a bell, think "color case hardening." Nobody does it better than Doug Turnbull, and his magnificent color case hardening is one of his signature touches.

A semiautomatic AR-type action is a considerable departure from, say, an 1876 Centennial Winchester. But unless you've been living in a very deep cave, you must recognize that this action and its many clones are currently the hottest-selling sporting arms in America. Yes, OK, some of this right now is "panic buying" out of concerns over potential legislation, but that doesn't explain why something like 90 manufacturers are making AR-type rifles. They are accurate, fun

to shoot, and in suitable calibers are appropriate to hunt with. I wouldn't go so far as to say that Doug Turnbull took a deep sigh and decided he should jump on the bandwagon. Actually, I know better. He thought about it long and hard, understanding that this type of rifle would be a major departure for both his reputation and his team. On the other hand, the hunger for this action type seems endless, and Turnbull thought he could put a slightly different spin on the AR ...after all, take a look at the acres and acres of metal on that action, just waiting to be case-hardened!

THE TURNBULL AR .308

MODEL: TAR-10

MANUFACTURER: Turnbull Manufacturing turnbullmfg.com

ACTION: Gas-operated Semiautomatic

BARREL: 16 in. Plus Muzzle Brake

OVERALL LENGTH: 37³/₈ in.

WEIGHT: 11¾ lbs.

STOCK: Premium American Walnut

METAL FINISH: Receiver–Color Case Hardened, Barrel & Fittings–Parkerized.

SIGHTS: None

MAGAZINES: 4- & 10-Round

SUGGESTED RETAIL: $4,995

Walnut, color case hardening, and classy lines are things not usually associated with AR-style rifles.

The 20th century meets the 21st century: Doug Turnbull with his gorgeous TAR-15.

THE TURNBULL AR

As they say, "parts is parts," and one of the attractive features of the AR platform is, after all, it's just parts that are largely interchangeable. The various companies that offer ARs generally source some components and manufacture others, depending on their own specialties and capacity. Turnbull is no different, except that to start with (in order to add that signature color case hardening) he has to have an all-steel receiver, both upper and lower. This adds weight. Against a sea of black synthetic stocks, another Turnbull difference almost had to be good walnut in both buttstock and hand-guard. This also adds a bit of weight.

The first (very small!) run of Turnbull ARs, including the rifle I shot and hunted with, are based on the larger 7.62/.308 Winchester AR-10 action. Even with a short 16.1-inch barrel, this is a heavy rifle, weighing 11¾ pounds empty without scope. Mind you, the AR-10 frame is always fairly heavy, so the steel receiver and walnut stock just add a bit extra. The weight makes it a real pleasure to shoot... but, regardless of how you feel about the capability and suitability of the .308 Winchester cartridge, this is probably not a rifle you'll want to carry up a sheep mountain. For stand hunting or any situation where you don't get too far from a horse or vehicle, no big deal. Nor is that frame size with attendant weight locked in concrete. The second (very small!) run of Turnbull ARs was on the smaller, lighter, and much more popular AR-15 frame. The initial chambering was .223, the standard and most popular AR-15 chambering.

The .223 is great for varmints and, where legal, OK for deer with heavy bullets, but today there are other options for hunting cartridges on the AR-15 frame, including 6.8mm SPC and .300 Whisper. Similarly, the .308 remains the standard and most popular chambering for the larger action (and there are no flies on it as a hunting cartridge), but other options include the full range of cartridges based on the .308 case, which includes .243 Winchester, 7mm-08 Remington, and .338 Federal. So the options are out there, and it's always hard to predict exactly what Doug Turnbull's adept little company is likely to do next.

In the meantime, out of a field of dozens of manufacturers making very similar rifles, the Turnbull AR is different. Although it comes at a price, it is not the most expensive AR on the market—but it might be among the most interesting. As always, Turnbull's color case hardening is incredible—and there's a lot of it! The walnut stock is simple but elegant, and the rifle has a Picatinny rail on top of the receiver,

ready for scope mounting, but without a factory-supplied rear sight. Functioning was perfect and accuracy was superb, but that shouldn't be sur-prising because, after all, there isn't much mystery remaining about this tried-and-true action.

Well, there weren't mysteries, but there were surprises. First, when I squeezed the trigger! Combine the short barrel with the muzzle brake/flash hider and this rifle is loud! I was glad my buck only needed one shot, and next time I swear I'll use hearing protection, even in the field! Second, I knew my deer season was limited, but I didn't know just how limited. That very afternoon I heard from Doug...the rifle I was using was the last of the first run. He had just sold it, so I needed to send it back immediately. And so I did...with considerable regret! Ⓗ

A Kiwi Whitetail

New Zealand's most difficult game.

Story & Photography by
Craig Boddington

It almost happened in the first 15 minutes of daylight. I was sitting a tree stand in a damp forest, straight out of *The Lord of the Rings*. The morning came slowly among the big, moss-hung trees. As the light came up, I tried to concentrate on the scrape that was almost visible among tall ferns. It was about a quarter past eight, very late but in this dark forest still very early, when I saw movement coming from the left.

It wasn't a Hobbit. It was a genuine whitetail. He came in with his head low, hidden by the ferns, but I was certain it was a buck. This was confirmed when he stopped and tended the scrape, just like a whitetail buck is supposed to do. Except now his head was exactly behind a thick tree. No problem. His body was clear, so

Although the author saw several white-tails from tree stands, he actually saw more just slipping through the woods at the right time of day.

I brought up the old .300 H&H and waited to see just a hint of antlers. Now he reached up for the mandatory overhanging branch, and I got a quick glimpse of ears on one side of the tree, nose on the other. However, there was something wrong; I got no hint of antlers with either view.

He obviously wasn't a big buck but he sure was going after that scrape like he was. New Zealand whitetails rarely grow large, and although this was my first morning, it wasn't my first hunt for these almost mythical forest creatures. I'd slogged through these damp hills before, enough to believe any buck was a pretty good trophy. So it wasn't like I intended to field-judge him—but I was worried his rack might be broken. I turned up the scope and waited. Sooner or later, he would have to step from behind the tree.

When he did, I wasn't certain whether to laugh or cry. He was a spike, just a big young-ster. What in the world a baby buck like that was doing scraping like the big boys I have no clue. In all the time I've spent hunting white-tails in North America I have never seen a buck so young tend a scrape—but I wasn't in North America.

Whitetails In New Zealand

Early settlers came into a land that was rich and green, but strangely devoid of large mammals. Through the latter part of the 19th and early years of the 20th Century they set about fixing that problem. Some of the releases were private, but most were more or less official under the auspices of regional "Acclimatization Societies." Most of us know about the stunning successes: Red deer, Himalayan tahr, and

The Glenorchy area, about an hour from Queenstown, is strikingly beautiful. The deer seem to hang out on the thickly wooded lower slopes coming out to the edges to feed.

Alpine chamois. Fallow deer are more localized, but well established in free-range herds. Still more localized, but definitely long established, are sambar, rusa, and sika deer. There were also some spectacular failures. American elk, *wapiti*, were introduced many years ago and at one point were well established in the

James Veint is third-generation in the Glenorchy area, and among New Zealand's few serious whitetail hunters. He believes in calling, and in search of whitetail knowledge is an avid reader of American hunting magazines—including this one.

South Island's rugged Fjordland. Over time, unfortunately, they crossbred with red deer, and there are probably not any pure wapiti remaining in the wild. Moose were also introduced into the same rugged wilderness, and were definitely established. It isn't clear what happened to them, probably overhunting since there has been little control of hunting of nonnative species. Decades have passed since there was a confirmed sighting. Other releases just never got off the ground. Five mule deer were released, but they vanished utterly. Himalayan blue sheep were also introduced, but were shot before they had a chance.

The whitetail is a different story. In the winter of 1904-1905 T.E. Donne and F. Moorehouse of the New Zealand Government Tourist & Health Resorts purchased 24 New Hampshire whitetails and took them on the 9,000-mile journey to New Zealand. Ultimately 18 animals survived the trip, and in late March 1905 were introduced into the wild through the Southland Acclimatization Society. Nine were released north of Lake Wakatipu. The other nine went to Stewart Island off the southern coast.

Both introductions were successful, in that, over a hundred years later, there remain viable populations of free-ranging whitetails. The Lake Wakatipu herd is very localized up the Dart and Rees River valleys. Limited habitat and unrestricted hunting have limited their growth throughout the 100 years; their entire range today is not much more than 15 miles east to west and possibly 30 miles north to south. There are probably just a few hundred whitetails in this herd. At long last there are restrictions on Crown land, and on private land more landowners are trying to protect their whitetails, so today they have a fighting chance.

The Stewart Island herd has fared better. It is brushy and lightly populated, and by the 1920s whitetails had spread into most of the suitable habitat. Today it's believed the Stewart Island whitetail herd numbers somewhere around

(Above) At the shot the buck ran and left no sign whatsoever. The author was certain it had gone into the trees, so he moved ahead slowly and there it was.

(Left) Introduced from New Hampshire in 1905, New Zealand's whitetails are of the northern woodlands subspecies, a good-sized deer with lots of color in the cape. This seven-pointer has some mass and character. He's not a monster—even by New Zealand standards—but he's a good one.

7,000 and in a recent year about 2,800 hunters took 1,400 deer. Note that this is "deer harvested;" mature bucks are just a small fraction of that number.

Right Place, Right Time

On the surface, then, it would seem Stewart Island is *the* place to hunt New Zealand's whitetails. Maybe, but it isn't quite so simple. Hunting on Stewart Island is by an allocated block system, making it difficult for an outsider to hunt there. Also, probably

because the browse and mineral conditions aren't ideal, Stewart Island whitetails are usually modest in the antler department. Whitetails are far fewer at Lake Wakatipu—but they grow reasonable racks and access is possible.

I made my first hunt in the South Pacific in 1988. Since then I have returned 15 times, and over the years I developed a perhaps silly goal of taking all the South Pacific species under free-range conditions. As such things go, some came easy and some hard. It took me two trips to take a hog deer on the coast of southern Australia. I also hunted sambar in the Australian state of Victoria and failed miserably. Of course, I got lucky here and there, and by 2006 just a couple of animals remained.

All my South Pacific friends and mentors, great hunters and friends had warned me. Sambar was difficult, but I could get one (sooner or later). The whitetail was the big problem. The consistent recommendation was the Lake Wakatipu herd, hunted out of Glenorchy, this because of access and potential antler size, not necessarily because of success. Success was low everywhere. Of the 14 South Pacific animals that can be hunted free range, the whitetail is consistently considered the most difficult. Yep, sure is.

Timing is a key issue in planning any hunt, but especially one 6,000 miles from home. Remembering that New Zealand's seasons are opposite, a common theory seemed to be these whitetails were best hunted in early autumn, March. The antlers are fully formed but the deer are still in heavy velvet, so they tend to go to the more open tops where they might be visible. In March 2006 Kiwi Safaris arranged for me to hunt with Glenorchy native James Mitchell, a good hunter and good guy—and we tried. Man, did we try. Although we climbed up there many times, we didn't find any whitetails on the tops. We found darned few along the miles of brush and thick forest that we slogged uphill through. There were deer. We found a

Although its' range is limited, sambar have been free-ranging on New Zealand's North Island since 1876. This is a nice stag, with typical three-tined antler and burly body. The rifle is a Remington M700 rebarreled to .300 H&H, topped with a Zeiss variable.

SERENDIPITOUS SAMBAR

WE HAD JUST taken a whitetail, South Pacific's most difficult creature. There are 14, and I had hunted them all, but not all successfully. One hurdle remained, the magnificent sambar, first introduced into New Zealand's North Island from Sri Lanka in 1876. I had tried and failed in Victoria Province, Australia, where the population is large and widespread—but never easy to hunt. With the whitetail secured more quickly than we dared hope, we rendezvoused at Chris and Peg's place. He knew a sheep farmer on the North Island, in sambar range, who said he had some. Should we give it a go?

So we flew to Palmerston North, where our new friend Greg Gower met us. Two hours later we were looking at a nice sambar stag. This seemed unbelievable, and I thought we should shoot him. We did not. After all, we had almost three days remaining to take the

South Pacific's greatest trophy—but only second-most after the whitetail in difficulty. Insanity!

The sambar lived in thick gorse brush in gulleys and canyons, coming into the open paddocks mostly at night—but the tropical deer they are, they stand up and feed in the brush when the sun shines. Except we caught yet another week of intermittent rain and cold wind. I was sure we had made a terrible mistake—and then, on the second afternoon, a pale sun popped, and so did the sambar. We found a good stag bedded on a little shelf with some hinds, bad angle and too much wind to take the shot from there. We circled around and above him, got a view, and waited a long time before I was confident of the shot. When I was sure, we shot him—a wonderful coal-black stag, and ended a 21-year South Pacific saga.

Contact: Chris Bilkey, (chrisbilkey@xtra.co.nz)

few rubs and saw a handful of does in a week of hard hunting—but never a buck.

Honestly, after that hunt I wasn't so sure about the whole thing. It seemed to me whitetails were so thin on the ground I was better off chasing unicorns. I looked into Stewart Island, but there was little opportunity for an outsider. It seemed pretty hopeless until my friend Chris Bilkey came up with a plan. Chris and his wife, Peg, have become good friends over the course of several hunts. While his specialty is South Island game, he has feelers out throughout the region. He didn't like the concept that a whitetail could beat us, so he started digging around.

He found James Veint, third-generation in the Glenorchy area, and one of New Zealand's very few serious whitetail hunters—he's probably taken more big New Zealand whitetails than anyone. His family farms north of Glenorchy, and has worked hard to protect their whitetails and let them build up. More than a year out James Veint suggested that the ideal time was May 18, 2009, and if I gave it a good week he could probably show me a buck.

Mid-May? That's the peak of the rut. Hunting at that time makes perfect sense to any American whitetail hunter, but Veint was the first New Zealander to suggest hunting during this time period. Chris Bilkey picked me up at the Queenstown airport, and we caught up a bit and checked my rifle enroute to Glenorchy. Then, whitetail hunting being a bit of a solitary sport, he left me in the good care of James and faded from the scene.

Rain And More Rain

That spike buck at dawn seemed a fortuitous omen. Later in the morning James came through to pick me up, and the little buck came back. Using his pale hand to imitate a tail flagging, he bleated him right in—and I knew, even more definitively than the mounted heads on his wall had shown, I was in the care of a real whitetail hunter. However, even a real whitetail hunter can't fight the weather. So far it had been an extremely wet fall, with the pastures waterlogged and the surrounding forests soaked. The rain continued, off and on, for the next two days.

We did the best we could, taking stands here and there, and still-hunting the ridges above the Veint pastures. We got wet, and we got tired fighting our way up rain-slick slopes. We never saw a branch-antlered buck, but we actually saw a lot of does and fawns and a couple more spike bucks. Better news, several of the does had twin fawns. The deer we saw weren't especially spooky; they were moving normally, and so long as we had the wind right we would see deer—at least, in between the rain showers.

On the third day the wind was finally favorable for James' best place, a high, forested bench where whitetails would be moving through in the morning. We climbed up in the dark, and, being terrified of heights, I baulked at a stand far up on a snag. So we moved on to an adjacent finger ridge 50 yards away, and again we saw deer, moving just as James had said they would, but no bucks. Then, it started to rain again.

Almost A Miracle

We lost most of the day to rain, but in the evening it cleared a bit and we took a walk along the forest fringe. That was an amazing evening; we got the drop on a dozen deer, the most I have ever seen, but not a single buck. We were running short on options. The time was right, but the weather was terrible, and the bucks James knew about around his farm had vanished, who knows why. Our next plan would be to take a helicopter up-country and get dropped off with a fly camp in some country James had hunted in previous seasons. I wasn't crazy about the chopper; it's been abused in New Zealand, although drop-off hunting is legal—but it seemed we needed some new country.

We set a helicopter pickup for the next afternoon, weather permitting. That evening, in the comfort of the Veint farmhouse, we organized our gear. We still had a morning hunt. We drove up the valley a ways, ditched the vehicle, and hiked across the fields to the edge of the dark timber. There were plenty of does along this edge, and by rights there should be a buck—but we just hadn't seen one. We didn't on this morning, although once again we saw plenty of does. It was late, and we had picked up the pace, heading back to the house, when we saw a lone whitetail still feeding out in the field, maybe 500 yards away across dead-open ground. From the body shape I knew it was a buck before we lifted the binoculars.

Yes, a buck, and a pretty good buck. However, he was unapproachable and there were a couple of low sheep fences between us. No way would I try that shot. We were hidden in the treeline, and in time he must make his way to us, either right or left.

He chose his right, our left, and he came fast. We ducked into the trees and jogged, our only chance to cut him off. We stopped at a fenceline, hoping for a shot, but we saw only his antlers above a low rise of ground. We scrambled over and hustled again, keeping just in the fringe of trees. To our right was some deadfall, beyond it the silhouette of a whitetail buck, walking toward the thick stuff. James and I heaved up against a big tree and I took a quick rest—but the deer was invisible. Then he stepped from behind a snag, walking fast. I swung with him, felt good and got the shot off.

There was no reaction. He vanished for a moment, then we saw him running away, over a little rise and gone. Wow, the shot felt fine, but I truly thought that, after all this, I had missed. We walked over the rise and found nothing, just open pasture beyond. To the left was thick timber. There were no clear tracks, no blood, but he must have ducked in there. We entered the trees and there he was, stone dead and absolutely beautiful. By North American standards he was a medium-sized buck—but I felt like I had taken a Boone & Crockett monster. Ⓗ

WESTERN PARADISE

MIKE SCHOBY

he country hadn't changed much in the decade since I had last seen it. The dust hung in the still evening air, giving the day a theatrical glow, and, after all of those years, I could still recognize the smell. Most places have a unique smell, and this place is no different. The basalt cliffs, craggy and black, were a stark contrast to the smooth, rolling, golden fields of wheat. In the valley below, the Palouse River tumbled by on its way through a progression of rivers, increasing in size before terminating at the Pacific Ocean, hundreds of miles away.

A clatter of rocks below shook me out of my wool-gathering, just in time to see a streak of brown hair tipped with mahogany antlers working its way up the volcanic chute in front of me. I smiled and readied my rifle.

WHEN A PLAN COMES together

The buck, who was soon to meet his demise, was the result of a plan coming together—something that seldom happens. Earlier in the day, we had seen several bucks disappear into the brush-choked hillside below the basalt cliff. Carl Lautenschlager, a good friend of nearly 20 years and the multi-generational owner of the ranch, wasn't surprised and said, "Yeah, those bucks always do that. They bed in the cuts and long grass breaks, and they will stay there all day. It's not easy to get them, but if some guys want to walk, we can do a push. We might have a chance of getting a shot at them when they squirt out the top."

Carl's brother, along with a couple others who had already tagged out, said they would walk, and the rest of us got situated on various pinnacles overlooking escape routes that spread out over the course of a half a mile.

I was perched on the rim of the basalt cliff along one of the main escape routes the deer had used for eons. The buck broke clear from the brush and stood perfectly still 80 yards away, looking back down the valley, trying to see the people who had rousted him from his bed. He was not huge, just a typical 8-pointer that is so common in this country. Since we were here for the fun of hunting and the delicious meat, not for wall-hangers, I centered the Leupold's crosshairs behind his shoulder and squeezed the Blaser's trigger. Chambered in .257 Weatherby, the 80-grain Barnes TTSX traveling at 3,800 fps instantly turned the lights out on the buck. I may have seen a deer die faster, but I honestly can't recall when. Dead on its feet, the deer tumbled back down into the valley.

A YEAR IN the MAKING

Like all great hunts, this one started a year before, when *HUNTING*'s Publisher, Kevin Steele, and I were deer hunting at Craig Boddington's place. We make it a point to get together once a year for a traditional deer camp. And while it is easy to say "traditional," there really is no such thing as a traditional deer camp. Hunts are as varied as the locale, people, and the season. This is a good thing. In fact, it is a great thing and is what makes deer hunting so enjoyable—the variety.

And no matter how good the current deer hunt is, you always yearn for your first deer hunt. For how you used to do it. For the way your father showed you. For the way your first deer looked.

So, after a few glasses of wine around the comfort of the crackling fire, we got to reminiscing about our first deer hunts. For Craig, Kansas called to him. He was born there, grew up there, and spent lots of memorable time hunting with his father there. Even though their early hunts were not deer hunts, places have a way of retaining memories, and Kansas holds a lot of memories for him.

Steele reminisced about blacktail in northern California. The season is early in the year, when it is hot and dry, so they hunted the early mornings before the heat got to be too much. The hunting sounded enjoyable, something to put on my mental bucket list.

Before I knew it, it was my turn to talk about my first whitetail hunt. Growing up in the West, my

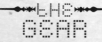

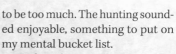

THE BASALT CLIFFS, CRAGGY & BLACK, WERE A STARK CONTRAST TO THE SMOOTH, ROLLING, GOLDEN FIELDS OF WHEAT.

While the rolling wheat fields provide abundant forage for whitetails, they also deliver a unique scene for hunting where hunters can watch partners stalk and shoot deer from afar, as we did with Kevin Steele and his buck.

story was a bit different. Most think of the West in terms of big mountains, elk, bear, mule deer, blacktails, and coyotes, and, while it is all of these things, much of the West is also littered with whitetails. And the hunting is like nothing I have experienced elsewhere.

Washington whitetail hunting is more like pheasant hunting combined with mule deer hunting than traditional Midwest whitetail hunting. The country is big and wide open, but the most notable difference is that hunting is done in groups. We would often start the day glassing from a high ridge as a group,

Once they bed, they generally stay put all day, not moving again until the last hour of light. So hunters pick the buck they want to try for and make a plan. Usually, the guy who first spotted the buck gets first right of refusal; in other cases, if someone who already tagged out spots a buck, it is open for anyone to go. It's all very informal and good-natured, and there are plenty of deer to go around.

QUANTITY VERSUS QUALITY

I was quick to tell Kevin that whitetail hunting in Washington is not about quality but quantity. Oh, occasionally a guy will knock down a buck that would be considered a bruiser by most standards, but that is not usually the case. Washington is about tonnage. You see, the Palouse region is wheat country interspersed by plum thickets, Russian olives, creeks, and long grass. Occasionally, a pine tree will dot a ridge, but for the most part it is open. Seeing dozens of deer is actually unremarkable; seeing hundreds is more common. But with numbers doesn't come size. If you go to the Palouse for a world record, you are going to be disappointed. But if you go there to get lots of action, have a fantastic communal hunt with buddies, and put some excellent venison in the freezer, you've gone to the right place.

Kevin said that sounded fantastic. Could he join the next year? Absolutely.

THE GROUP HUNT

Since I was tagged out after the first evening drive, I would be on the spotting and driving crew. So the second morning we all gathered around a haystack on one of the highest points of Carl's prop-

WASHINGTON WHITETAIL HUNTING IS ABOUT QUANTITY. WHILE TROPHIES ARE RARE, THE NUMBERS OF DEER ARE STAGGERING.

anywhere from a couple of guys to the whole camp of a dozen or more. It is a family and friends hunt, so competition is not a concern. The glassing sessions would turn into fun, joking times sipping coffee while focusing binoculars and spotting scopes on the far, distant ridges.

For the first couple hours after light, deer can be seen moving in small groups. They feed on the wheat and alfalfa at night and move back to the protective basalt cliffs, brushy thickets, and long grass along the creek to wait out the rest of the day. A typical morning of glassing will show hundreds of deer with several shooter bucks.

erty. From there you can see miles and spot deer in every direction. We hadn't been at it long when I spotted a buck already bedded a quarter-mile away in a small eyebrow just off the crest of the hill.

"You want to go for him?" I asked Kevin as we looked the buck over in the morning sun.

"He is in a pretty decent place to stalk," Kevin replied. "I could go around the back side of the hill, the wind is right, and come right over the top on him." Kevin was thinking as he spoke. "Yeah, I'll give him a shot." With that he grabbed two cameramen and headed out.

It was the better part of half an hour before we saw Kevin clear the horizon behind the bedded deer, but several hundred yards off to the south, unaware of exactly where he marked him before he began the stalk. It is so common; something that looks easy from afar is seldom easy when you get close. Looking through binoculars, we frantically tried to get Kevin's attention, but the distance was too great and he was focused on locating the buck.

Luckily, he realized his mistake before fully cresting the ridge, and we watched with relief as he backed up and worked north a couple hundred yards before popping back over the ridge, this time right on top of the buck. The buck, still unaware of Kevin's presence, remained bedded, looking over the large wheat field in front of him.

With breaths held, we watched intently as the distance between Kevin and the buck shrank to near spitting distance. Of course, objects appear closer together through magnification than they are in reality, but he was close, and, due to the hillside, neither was completely sure of the other's location, Finally, through binoculars, we saw the buck jump out of his bed at a full run. Dust appeared in the field, and a second later we heard the shot roll across the distance. At about the same time, the buck staggered and went down.

"That was awesome!" my hunting buddy, Taro Sakita, said. "There are not many places you get to see a guy stalk and shoot a deer."

My brother, Greg, still looking through a spotting scope at a ridge nearly a mile away in the other direction, said absentmindedly, "Well, it looks like you all are going to get another show. I just saw two decent bucks slip off the top of that wheat field and bed below that basalt cliff. Both were shooters. Taro, you want to go with me?"

Greg and Taro grabbed their rifles, loaded up in Taro's truck, and took off, planning to go the several miles around the Palouse River the long way and come in on the backside of the wheat field before getting out to make their stalk.

A half hour later, we watched through spotting scopes as they crested the far horizon above the bedded bucks. We could no longer see the pair of bucks, as they had sunk down in the deep grass, too well hidden to spot, but there were limited ways out of their bedding area, and none of us had seen them sneak out. Odds were good that they were still there.

Greg and Taro crept to the top of the basalt butte and peered over.

It wasn't long until we saw Greg lie prone and ready his rifle. A single shot drifted across the distance. A buck jumped out of the long grass and ran down the slope toward the river. Through the spotting scope, we watched Taro sit down and get into position over shooting sticks. Greg's buck must have been down, and this was the second buck. The deer crossed the river and stopped to look back at the duo. That was his fatal mistake. A shot rang out from Taro's .257 Roberts, and the buck found out that even 392 yards away wasn't quite far enough. Hit hard, he stumbled into a brush pile where he died.

the camp

That night at our wall tent camp, sitting around a crackling fire, grilling steaks, and listening to the Palouse River gurgle by, we talked about the last couple of days. Of our group, Steele, Monte Milanuk from Savage Arms, my brother, Taro, and I had all taken bucks. Carl's brother had shot a buck, as had a young family friend and Carl's daughter. All told, in three short days we took eight deer. By the end of the week, between Carl's family and a few clients Carl let in, 18 deer were taken, making for 100-percent success in nine days...pretty amazing numbers anywhere. But more than the deer, this hunt reminded me of why I love hunting whitetails in the West. It is the joking, the fun, the camraderie, the tents, and the open fires. It is eating chunks of backstrap hot off the grill with your fingers until you can't fit another morsel into your mouth, then collapsing on a cot while the wood stove works its way through a piece of pine. It was that yearly tradition that few other experiences can ever match and one I will be happy to do again and again. ◉

10 CLASSIC RUT STRATEGIES THAT STILL WORK

BACK 2 BASICS

DAVID DRAPER

IF THERE'S ONE thing hunters are good at, it's taking the fun out of the woods. Let's use deer hunting as an example. We've become so laser-focused on killing the biggest buck in the woods, a whole industry has developed around hunting the rut. I'll even gladly take some of the blame. Writers are famous for overcomplicating things, but in truth, today's deer aren't all that different from those hunted a half-century ago; there are just a lot more of them. So this season, forget the hype and go back to the classic strategies our fathers and grandfathers taught us 20 or more years ago. Here are 10 well-worn rut strategies that still work.

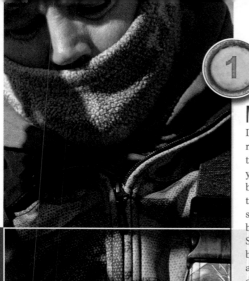

1

MAKE SCENTS

Deer scents have taken a beating in recent years, with deer "experts" discounting their effectiveness and states (we're looking at you Virginia and Vermont) banning urine-based deer attractants over fears they may transmit chronic-wasting disease. CWD is serious enough that I won't argue that point, but I can speak from experience to the former: Scents are in fact deadly effective. The first buck I killed, a tall 9-pointer, came running in and stopped on a dime to stick his nose in the dirt where I poured a drop of Tink's #69. Since then, I've had plenty of bucks—and does, too—nose their way down a drag line. If bucks use their olfactory glands to find hot does, it only stands to reason that a good-quality doe-in-heat scent should bring bucks in. Try this classic strategy: Dip a hank of fabric in doe pee, tie it to your boot, and walk to your stand. Make a big circle, then refresh the wick with more pee and hang it on a shooting lane. Chances are, any buck that crosses that path will follow it right to your stand.

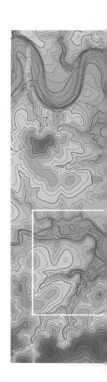

4

IT'S NOT A LOCK

In recent years, it's become vogue to talk about the lockdown, that period during the rut when a buck finds a hot doe and never leaves her side. But do deer really vanish in mid-November? No way. While a buck may lock on to a receptive doe for a day, they don't disappear altogether, and that doe will still do her best to feed regularly. No, it's not the deer that's locked down. It's you. Most likely you're hunting the same spot you scouted in October, and the deer have moved on to a peak-rut pattern where they're covering a lot more ground. Bucks are also moving at different times, with increased activity after dark and more midday movement.

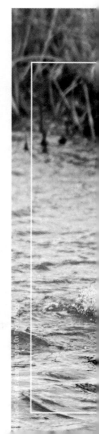

2 IN A PINCH

Hunters spend a ton of their time scouting for rubs and scrapes, but if they took the time to look at the big picture, they'd find most of the sign is located in pinch points. That's because bucks like to lay sign where other deer will come across it, and these land forms, whether they're necked-down woods or high-country saddles, funnel deer into a concentrated spot as they travel. Instead of tromping through the woods, spooking every animal in the process, sit at the kitchen table with a beverage close at hand and pore over topo maps and aerial photographs of your hunting area. Find these pinch points and I promise there will be deer sign and the bucks that made it nearby.

3 GO TO GROUND

Hunters lying in wait in the treetops for a deer to wander by is a relatively recent phenomenon, especially for those of you who don't believe in evolution. Fact is, a lot of deer were killed well before the first modern treestand came on the market in the 1960s. In the big woods, where there is a lot of ground to hunt, and areas where deer density is low, still-hunting is a deadly effective rut strategy. Find a hillside and slowly stalk parallel to the ridge-line, or go for broke and slip into the thickest cover you can find in hopes of catching a rut-worn buck while he's napping. Sneaking through standing corn is another great tactic when bucks are sparring along field edges.

5 WATERWORKS

Bucks may not take a lunch break during the rut, but they do have to hydrate. They're smart about it, however. Think like a horny college kid, which you probably once were. What's the best bar for an eligible bachelor looking to score? The one with a popular ladies' night. Same goes for bucks. They're visiting water-holes the does are using most and checking them frequently throughout the day. Do some scouting and find a seep, pond, or other water located between a food source and bedding area. Chances are the banks are beaten down with tracks, and usually there's a well-trod path clueing you into the preferred approach. Rivers and creeks may have more than just one watering spot, but bucks love to cruise these corridors until they find a hot trail. Set up accordingly.

6

CALLING ALL DEER

When it comes to deer calls, hunters have seen it all—from the phlegmatic grunt-snort-wheeze that sounds more like Grandpa than a goliath buck to, and I'm not joking here, a call mimicking the sound of a feeder throwing corn. No doubt both of those, and the myriad of other calls on the market, can bring in a buck but, from my experience, not with regularity. One call that deer will almost always investigate is the fawn bleat. Most often it's does that come running—that maternal instinct is too strong to ignore—but bucks also will come to a fawn bleat, though usually with more caution. I keep a grunt tube handy, but a flip-over style bleat can is my go-to call all season long.

7

HIGH NOON

Every hunter knows sitting all day is one of the best ways to tag a rutting buck, but that common knowledge is rarely followed by anyone but the most dedicated. Why? Because sitting on stand from an hour before sunup to well after sundown sucks. So sleep in instead. Sure, bucks are running like mad men early and late, but they actually do more cruising during the midday hours as they move between known bedding areas, trying to bump a hot doe from her resting place. Hang a stand adjacent to bedding areas or along funnels that connect several areas of thick cover and save it for the peak of the rut. Just be on alert on approach as those same cruising bucks can easily bust hunters as they walk in.

8

STAY HOME

Popular thought would have you believe a buck abandons his home range at the first whiff of a hot doe. Wrong. Studies tracking GPS-collared bucks have shown that even when the chasing and seeking phases are at their peak, bucks don't stray far from home. When they do happen to go for a walkabout in search of a doe willing to stand, they don't stay gone long. If you've got a particular buck you're hunting, identify his core territory and build a strategy to hunt him at home. The biggest bucks are the ones that are the smartest, having survived several hunting seasons. They know where they feel the safest, and when hunters invade the woods, which they do in droves in November, a smart buck will retreat to safety rather than breed.

10

A GIRL'S GOTTA EAT

Studies have shown bucks can lose nearly a third of their body weight in the chasing and seeking phase of the rut, but you know who's not missing the dinner bell? Does. Despite the harassment they're receiving from over-eager bucks, the ladies are still hitting their preferred food sources throughout late October and November. After all, they need to be in the best shape possible to handle the months between peak conception and fawn drop. Follow the does to alfalfa, bean, and corn fields or along isolated oak ridges, where they're keying on leftover mast, and set-up downwind if possible. I guarantee bucks won't be far away as they scent check the area for any does that might be starting estrous.

9

LADIES FIRST

Consider this the "tl;dr rule"—as in, too long, didn't read. Almost every rut rule, including all those listed here, is predicated not by the behavior of the buck that hunters try so hard to decipher, but by what the does are doing. After all, it's no so secret that women really rule the world, and all of us guys are just living in it. Put some time and research into what the does in your hunting area are doing and I promise you'll be well on the way on tagging a trophy buck.

For everyone who watches The Weather Channel before traveling to a hunting destination.

By Jim Bequette

While packing my bags for a trophy whitetail hunt last winter, I flipped on The Weather Channel and saw this strange graphic hovering over the state of Kansas and other parts of the Midwest All those glowing orangeish, greenish, reddish, yellowish colors—something I don't think I had ever seen regarding a fast-moving winter weather-related storm. Translated, the very fluid, flowing and swirling colors represented this projection: Kansas was targeted as being in the path of one of the worst ice storms in state history.

I immediately started unpacking my bags and repacking more insulated clothing and gear, being mindful of the ice storm predictions now running across the bottom of the television screen and how the layering of clothing and heavier, insulated boots could really pay off on this five-day whitetail hunt

Leupold's Mike Slack and I were headed to outfitter Larry and Becky Olmstead's place in Hiawatha, Kansas, called Thunder Valley Lodge, which is nestled in some of the best whitetail country I have ever seen. A mix of hardwoods, corn fields, river and creek bottoms made up a patchwork quilt of ideal white-tail habitat. And this country, without question, held some of those "monster" trophy whitetails we've all been hearing about. Kansas has truly become a destination point for trophy deer hunters, certainly as much as the states of Illinois or Iowa have become whitetail hotspots.

Upon our arrival, Mike and I looked toward the low-ceiling gray skies and acknowledged that the wind that was swirling and blowing out of the northwest was going to bring a radical change to the weather conditions in the area we would be hunting and ultimately prove The Weather Channel was right on target with its forecast. In fact, as we drove from the Kansas City airport to north-central Kansas, I had taken note of a couple of abandoned farmsteads where several old Aermotor windmills were spinning like crazy.

But our thoughts turned from the weather to trophy whitetails once we entered Larry and Becky's lodge. Several big deer were mounted on the walls, and he had some whitetail sheds that provided an adrenaline rush that made it difficult to fall asleep that first night in anticipation of what we could see at first light. The sheds also took our thoughts away from the weather—at least temporarily.

Even sighting-in our rifles—Kimber Model 8400s—became a lot more difficult, as the wind and cold quickly took its toll on exposed skin while trying to zero-in our rifles with what amounted to about a 35-mile-per-hour cross wind. We managed to accomplish what turned out to be a real chore, and were both confident after targeting our Kimbers that if a buck made the fatal mistake of showing himself, that day would be his last.

Morning brought more frigid and dropping temperatures, along with an even stronger wind that cut through us like a knife. The good news was that we were being situated in elevated but enclosed box blinds, out of the wind. It helped a great deal, as I don't think we could have spent any time in the field in the open due to the icy conditions that continued to deteriorate.

As predicted, it started snowing, and then the snow turned to ice. The wind picked up and sang through the window openings in the blinds. Deer movement was bound to be impacted. But we took the positive approach and figured the abrupt weather change would kick the deer out of their beds and get them mov-ing to feed. We maintained this positive approach the first day, and we did see deer movement, but it was of smaller bucks and a multitude of feisty does.

To counterattack the elements, Larry's strategy was to remain in some blinds and rotate to blinds in morning or evening that would take us out of the wind or look out over a natural funnel. The strategy made sense, but the weather proved to be something we simply couldn't overcome.

The storm moved in full throttle the next evening, and everything iced up. From scraping the truck windows in the morning to layering to the max to crunch-ing through the ice and snow on our way to stand destinations, it became ever so clear that the weather had dramatically impacted our hunting—and ultimately dampened our hopes. Ice covered everything, sticking even to our rifles and optics and our packs. It truly was a winter wonderland, all the glistening ice that covered abandoned farm buildings and even the knee-high grasses and corn stalks we weaved our way through to and from the stands each morning and evening.

There was now no denying that the wintry conditions translated to minimal deer movement. It's almost as if the bucks sensed that something big was about to happen weatherwise and holed up in the bottoms, ready to ride out what turned out to be the storm of the century for Kansas. The few deer that did move literally had coats of ice and snow on their backs. They'd shake themselves to try and remove some of the extra weight frozen solid to their backside, but to little or no avail.

Nevertheless, Mike and I, along with Larry and his guides, remained commit-ted to the hunt, with the hope that the big bucks would start moving. And we were impressed with the way they all went about their business. I've been on guided hunts where at the first drizzle of rain or the first few flurries of snow, the guide/outfitter will either not go out in the morning or cut the hunt short in the evening to get back to the warmth of the lodge. As my uncle always used to tell me, "You can't kill a deer while sitting at the kitchen table drinking a cup of coffee." But with each passing hour and day our hopes sank a little more, as the storm had now escalated to the point that it seemed everything was locked down. There was very little traffic on the country roads, as the icy conditions made for hazardous driving, and it seemed as if all the wildlife in the country—from songbirds to coyotes to deer—had heard about The Weather Channel forecasts and decided to bed down and ride out the storm in the thickest cover available.

Larry and his guides kept up the good fight, and it finally paid off for Mike. The evening of the next-to-last day of the hunt, Mike was overlooking a huge cornfield that laid in a bottom that was bound on one side by a creek and on the other by a high ridge that clearly was a natural funnel for deer movement. The food source was there, as was the cover, and there were plenty of does to entice a buck to show himself.

Deer movement was reduced by the coming storm—it was like the deer knew the storm of the century was over the horizon.
Photo Credit: Jim Bequette

It turned out one buck decided to shake the ice and snow off his back and come down off that ridge to look over the does and feed before the worst of the storm hit the area. But as big bucks typically do, he waited until the last light of day to make his move into the cornfield. Mike showed his patience by remaining alert throughout the afternoon and evening in miserable conditions.

His patience paid off when he spotted the buck. The problem was, he was almost all the way on the other side of the cornfield—and by Mike's estimate, a good 400 yards from the treestand he and his guide were in.

The guide told Mike the buck was a shooter, and he wanted to know if he felt comfortable shooting at such along distance. An avid hunter with plenty of field experience in North America and Africa, Mike was clearly confident in his Kimber chambered for .270 WSM, the Federal 140-grain factory load and, of course, his choice of optics—Leupold's VX-L 3.5-10Xx50mm scope, which has outstanding light-gathering qualities. As it turned out, the scope he had mounted on the rifle made the difference between taking the shot and passing on it. Without that scope and the 50mm objective, there would have been no shot.

He quickly sized up the situation, placed his cheek against the stock and in extremely low-light conditions where the true value of light-gathering optics can save a hunt, Mike placed the Duplex crosshairs on the buck's vitals and ever so carefully squeezed the trigger.

At the rifle's report, the buck jumped and bolted. He clearly had been impacted hard in die vitals. He didn't go far, before he disappeared into the cut cornstalks.

Mike accepted congratulations from his guide, got down out of the stand, turned on his flashlight and anxiously crossed the field to take a closer look at this trophy. By the time he reached the buck it was totally dark. His guide had es-

Mike Slack with his Kansas buck right before the weather went from bad to worse.
Photo Credit: Jim Bequette

timated the shot at about 425 yards. The buck's vitals were destroyed. It was quite a testimony to Mike's skills as a rifleman and the Federal ammunition, Kimber rifle and Leupold scope. It was an extremely difficult shot he had made, and he now had a 140-class buck to take home. It was a classic example of how confidence in rifle, scope and ammo can make all the difference in the world in this type of hunting situation,

I'm sure the weather didn't seem nearly as frigid and the ice not as slick or bothersome after Mike downed that Kansas buck. Things always look better and brighter after your trophy is hanging in the meat locker.

For me, the weather was worsening. The wind picked up a notch, the ice and snow was coming down almost at a horizontal level, and it was almost unbearable for humans and game animals. The deteriorating conditions brought the realization that there will always

be another opportunity to hunt Kansas whitetails and that there was no need to risk our safety and ignore the inevitable: The weather conditions were worsening, and as the old saying goes, we needed to "get out of Dodge"—how appropriate...

Of course, I was disappointed in not seeing a shooter buck. The frustrating part was I knew they were there. The scrapes and rubs we saw were a clear indication that some huge whitetails made this area their home; Larry and his guides had done their job and scouted the area thoroughly. They knew the movement patterns of those big bucks but unfortunately, the inclement weather changed everything, and the deteriorating conditions quickly tinned dangerous and had convinced the bucks not to leave their beds—as we did each and every morning.

But as with every hunt, it's the comraderie, the friendship that counts when another hunter in camp takes a deer, and all of us gathered around the evening after

Mike knocked down his buck with an extraordinary shot and toasted him, his shot and his trophy. We exchanged more deer hunting stories late into the night as the wind howled and the ice pelted the windows of the lodge.

There were no regrets. We definitely made the right decision to leave when we did, as the storm only escalated. I heard from Larry several days later, and he told me the storm had forced him and his wife to batten down the hatches and lay low for almost a week-long period. His electricity had gone out, and area power and phone lines were down; fortunately, he had a generator as a backup power source. The conditions were truly life-threatening. The snow and ice storm turned ugly, and the power outages and drifting caused by high winds resulted in impassable roads, and ultimately many area residents were forced from their homes or had to be rescued.

The hunt took on a different perspective. We were reminded once again that no matter how well prepared you are when planning a hunt, Mother Nature can play havoc with your plans. Mike and I were grateful for the opportunity to hunt big whitetails in Kansas, and we hopefully will return to hunt with Larry, who was most gracious about inviting us back to give it another shot. We knew the deer were there, the cover was exceptional, and Larry ran a top-flight camp with top-drawer guides—that's all you can ask of a hunting outfit. Unfortunately, no outfitter, no matter how good, can control the weather. Ⓗ

SECTION TWO
WHITETAIL SAVVY

BIG BUCK LESSONS

FOR EVERY BIG BUCK TAGGED, THERE'S A STORY AND A LESSON TO BE LEARNED.

(L to R) Jeff Danker, Aaron Volkmar and buddy Matt Duff with Danker's late season, sub-zero bruiser.

EVERY HUNTER LOVES to hear a story about a big buck, particularly the one that didn't get away. In fact, with today's digital media able to send photos and stories of big deer from the very spot the animal dropped, news of a trophy being tagged often travels faster than the lucky hunter can get it out of the woods. As interesting as each of these stories are, the tale often goes a little deeper than one of pure entertainment— there's usually a lesson to be learned to apply to your own hunt the next time you climb into your stand. Here are three hunter's stories from the 2009 season and the lessons they have to share.

Know Your Geography

The Tale: The country was gripped in one of the worst cold spells it had experienced in more than a decade, and the Midwest was enduring the brunt of it. Jeff Danker, of Buckventures Outdoors television, was hunting with Iowa outfitter Aaron Volkmar. It was the late muzzleloader season in early January. With daytime temperatures in the negative teens and more than two feet of snow on the ground, Danker wasn't as worried about not seeing a nice buck as he was that when he did, the cold would have made it already drop its antlers.

"We knew with the weather the deer would be feeding like crazy, but we were worried about the antlers dropping," Danker says. To make matters worse, there was more bad weather on the way.

Suited up in Heater Body Suits, Danker and his cameraman set up off a 40-acre field of standing corn. The deer were yarded up in big herds and with the cold, they had been pounding the easy food source hard.

"With the corn still standing, a lot of deer were just bedding in there and eating throughout the day," Danker says. "The funny thing is as the afternoon wore on, the deer that had bedded in the surrounding woods, came to feed in the corn, and the deer in the corn went into the brush." That first afternoon, he spotted a bruiser buck that would measure in the 160s. But the whitetail was too far away and never presented a shot.

Pinpointing where the buck had exited the woods, the next afternoon, Danker set up closer to that spot being sure to keep the wind in his face.

It was almost dark when the big buck strolled out in almost the same spot where it had the day before. Danker took aim with his Traditions muzzleloader and made the 70-yard shot. It was his first big Iowa muzzleloader buck and measured an impressive 162 inches.

The Lesson: Most hunters live and die by the rut, going about the late season in a haphazard fashion. But the fact is, big bucks are still out there, and after a tiring rut period, they need to feed in order to get their strength back up. As deer begin to herd up, they feed voraciously on available foods such as standing corn. If you own or lease land where you can plant food plots, be sure to plant some corn, beans or sweet-tasting *brassicas*. If you can, don't hunt those plots until the end of the season. The combination of food and no pressure will put deer at ease, enticing them into the open while it is still light.

Steve Jarvis had jumped up this 17-point Virginia buck several times in the same spot while coyote hunting the year before. He returned during the opening week of firearms season and scored.

Another crucial lesson here was Danker's clothing. When temperatures plummet, deer will move, but you've got to be out there and to do that, you have to be able to keep warm and sit still. Even if you only wear them several days out of the season, invest in some good cold-weather gear. It could make the difference in filling that buck tag or ending the season empty handed.

Scout Late

The Tale: Virginia's Steve Jarvis is serious about his hunting. Each year, Jarvis takes four weeks off in the fall to coincide with the last three weeks of bow season and the first week of gun season—basically from mid-October through mid-November. During this vacation period, Jarvis hunts every day. He typically spots several deer each week that he is eager to arrow and frequently gets a chance at a nice buck or two each season.

But 2009 was different. The oaks' shed their plentiful acorns early and bucks didn't have to move far from their bedding areas to feed. Even as the rut began to ramp up, many deer kept to the woods with little need to expose themselves in open fields.

"I never shot at a buck during bow season," Jarvis says. "I passed some small deer and only saw two I would have shot."

Needless to say, by the time the opening week of gun season rolled around, a frustrated Jarvis knew he only had another good week of hunting left before it was back to work. Following last year's deer season, Jarvis had been out coyote hunting several times when he jumped up a huge buck from its bed.

Each time, the buck had been in the same general spot. He wondered if that deer was still bedding there. With nothing else working, he decided to give it a try.

Just before 9 a.m., he caught the buck slipping through the woods headed for the very spot where he had jumped him the year before. A well-placed shot from his slug gun dropped the 17-point, 168-inch buck.

The Lesson: Deer season may be over, but that doesn't mean it's time to pack it all in and sit by the fire. Whether you go after predators or small game or are simply doing a little post-season scouting, get out there and check those haunts you were afraid to traipse through during deer season. This is the time to inventory the bucks on your land that survived the season and try to figure out where the heart of their home range lays. Note key sightings and remember them when next season rolls around and you plan your stand locations.

Make Some Noise

The Tale: It was down to desperation time—the last day of

The author shot this split-brow 12-pointer on the final day of an Oklahoma muzzleloader hunt after catching the buck's attention with a rattling bag.

a five-day blackpowder hunt in western Oklahoma. I was hunting with Rick White, pro-staffer for Hunter's Specialties, who had taken an impressive 9-pointer early in the hunt. I had passed on an 8- and a 10-point earlier in the week that would have strained to reach 130 inches. The day before, perched on a wind-swept hillside, Rick and I had watched as a huge-bodied buck in the company of four other deer turned and walked back into the drainage from where he had appeared as the others all fed past our position a mere 80 yards away.

Like the morning before, the big buck emerged from the same creekbed less than a half-hour after sunrise. But this time, he set off on the trail of three does that had exited the drainage and headed for a block of woods more than 300 yards to our left. We watched helplessly as the buck prepared to disappear into the distant trees, when Rick asked if I had my rattle bag with me.

"Sure," I replied.

"Hand it to me, quick," Rick said as I pulled the noisemaker from my daypack. He quickly mashed the rods inside the bag together, mimicking two bucks fighting. The big buck paused, looked our way and then bounded into the cover.

"Oh well, it was a worth a try," I told him. "Maybe he'll come back," Rick nodded.

Not 20 minutes later, Rick excitedly told me to get ready. The buck had just emerged from the tree line and was heading for the ravine that stretched below our perch. I scrambled to settle the .50-caliber T/C, and though the buck dropped into the ravine and emerged in a spot that put him just over 150 yards away (instead of the 80 I had anticipated), the gun was up to the task. I angled the shot into the quartering away deer. He buckled and made a dash for the distant cover. The shot looked good but we waited before following him up. We found him expired in a creek two hours later. The 12-pointer with split brows scored 143 inches.

The Lesson: Never accept that the hunt is over just because a deer is heading away from your stand, particularly during the prerut and rut when they are more susceptible to calling. Make some noise, grunt or rattle antlers. Cast out some bleats from a can, anything to catch his attention and make him curious, angry or both. A hunt that seems like it's about to go down the drain, can turn your way with a little determined effort. ▣

Crushed Velvet

Want a trophy more rare than a big rack, a drop tine or split brows? Try hunting a buck in velvet.

"I consider myself the king of the August hunt," says Peter Simmons. Bold words for sure, but it's probably pretty close to accurate given the fact that the outfitter's lodge is located near the town of Estill in the heart of South Carolina's Low Country. The region is the only place in the United States where a deer hunter can pursue whitetails in August, a time when bucks are still sporting velvet on their racks. Last year, in those first two weeks of prime velvet time Simmons hosted 48 hunters at his lodge. They tagged 51 bucks.

What truly sets apart the state is that deer hunters aren't limited to archery tackle like sportsmen in other areas where some September seasons begin early enough to catch a buck with fuzzy antlers. There's no warm-up period in the Low Country. There, firearms are on tap from the word "Go," making the Palmetto State the number-one option for a hunter looking to tag a velvet whitetail—and not just in August.

DESTINATION SOUTH CAROLINA

To hunters used to being limited to a single buck tag or, even worse, having to draw for one, South Carolina is a potential paradise. Graced with an abundant—in some cases overabundant—deer population, the state boasts one of the longest, most liberal bag limits of any place whitetails roam. In the counties of Beaufort, Charleston, Berkeley, Dorchester, Colleton, Jasper, Hampton, Allendale, Bamburg, Barnwell, Orangeburg, Calhoun, Aiken, Richland and Lexington, there is no limit on bucks. Does are limited to two per day on either-sex days. If you purchase bonus tags (and you can buy as many as you want), you can erase from your mind any concern about doe days.

So why the ridiculously early start date? From the state's earliest times, hunting deer with dogs was a huge tradition that kicked off each year around mid-August. As South Carolina, like many states, moved to establish a department of natural resources in the early 1900s, Low Country legislators, fearful such an agency would take away their traditional start date, passed legislation establishing the permanent opening day. The Low Country whitetail season dates are the only ones not established by the S.C. Department of Natural Resources.

Tennesse hunter Robert Fife scored on this trophy velvet whitetail near Estill, South Carolina, in 2009. South Carolina hunters can expect to see bucks in the 120-class range, though trophies in the 140s and 150s are always possible.

South Carolinian Josh Robbins didn't have to travel far for his velvet-rack whitetail, taken last August.

insects, August hunters must focus on food areas to score on trophy whitetails.

"You can forget everything you know about rattling and grunting and all that when you come down here," says Simmons. "These deer are locked on feeding patterns at this time of year, still trying to grow their antlers before they begin rubbing them.

"Here in South Carolina, deer at this time are mostly attracted to soybeans and even cotton. They won't eat the cotton itself, but they will eat cotton leaves in their younger state. Some cornfields are also harvested in August, which can really help out a hunter."

The majority of Low Country deer hunting is done over large crop fields or food plots to take advantage of this natural tendency of deer to head to the fields in late summer to feed. Average shots can run between 250 and 300 yards, requiring a steady rest and a nice, flat-shooting rifle/caliber combination. High-powered rifle-scopes, as well as binoculars, can also be advantageous. In the event of corn being cut early, Simmons says that is a golden opportunity.

"The minute that combine shuts down, you want to be in that field or even in the cab of that combine itself," he says. As in most places, the deer here are oblivious to any danger from agricultural operations, associating the presence of heavy equipment with the available food it creates after it runs through a field.

PARADE OF BUCKS

Another aspect of August hunting that can really be helpful is the fact that bucks are still roaming and feeding in bachelor groups. There's a real chance that when a big boy strolls into the open, he won't be alone. He'll likely have two, three, four or even more like-sized bucks in his company, providing an opportunity to size up what the local herd has to offer. Don't do anything to disturb them and odds are they'll keep coming back every day, giving you a chance to get in optimal position for a shot at the deer of your choice.

"The key is to shoot one and shoot him dead where you don't have to track and trail him through the woods disturbing everything," says Simmons. If you can pull it off, you can come back to that same spot the very next day and in all likelihood shoot another one.

"It's a great time to kill a quality deer," he adds.

MORE OPTIONS

While the early gun season in South Carolina is without peer in the whitetail world for velvet opportunities,

Before some Midwestern hunter starts going *ga-ga* over all this coastal opportunity, there's a slight downside (isn't there always?). The weather in August is downright hellish, with typical days soaring into the mid-90s, and buzzing insects swarm every living creature with a tenacity generally reserved for angry wives trying to argue their side of an issue. (A ThermaCell is a must, though it won't help you with the wife.) The warm climate translates into generally smaller-bodied deer, and eight-pointers are more the norm than beastly nontypical bucks of 10 points or more. An average shooter buck is going to run in the 120-inch ballpark, with 130s totally possible. Some 140s and 150s are taken each season, with larger deer being much more rare but not unheard of.

One of Simmons' hunters shot a 154-inch buck last year. You simply don't get the mass common to bucks found in states such as Illinois, Iowa, Wisconsin and Kansas. What you do get is a great chance to take a buck in velvet. Try doing that in Indiana, or most other states for that matter.

THE TRICK TO SUMMER BUCKS

"August is my favorite time to hunt," says Simmons. "Deer have not been shot at, they haven't been harassed or disturbed in any way. They are completely at ease, which makes them easier to hunt." However, there is still a trick. Besides contending with the heat and biting

HANDLE WITH CARE

Because a velvet rack is in all likelihood just days or weeks away from being rubbed clean by its owner, special care must be taken to avoid damaging the rack before you get it to a taxidermist. David Sichik, owner of Real Deal Taxidermy in New Jersey, suggests hunters use a four-wheeler if at all possible to remove a velvet-rack buck from the woods to avoid damaging the sensitive covering. From there, freeze it as quickly as possible. Whatever you do, don't drag this deer out of the woods like you would with one shot in November.

Avoid handling or squeezing the rack as much as possible while caping the hide, and don't let it drag on the skinning room floor. If you have to ship the head to your taxidermist, freeze it, pack it with cushioning materials and mark it as fragile when shipping. If at all possible, drive it to your taxidermist yourself.

Pete Simmons says his guides load velvet bucks straight into the truck whenever possible. Each one also carries blankets to wrap the antlers. Once at the taxidermist, he will likely inject the velvet with formaldehyde or similar chemical to preserve the outer covering and keep it as natural as possible.

the state doesn't hold a monopoly on such bucks. Although whitetails tend to begin rubbing their antlers free of velvet beginning in early September, there are a number of states such as North Dakota, Montana, Minnesota, Delaware and even Georgia that have bow-only seasons that come early enough that you can potentially catch a buck in velvet still roaming the woods.

Go farther north and you will find outfitters in Alberta offering bowhunts for whitetails in velvet. There, while a hunter might be limited because of the bow-only restriction, deer size will hardly be an issue like it may be for sportsmen who hail from states where giants are common.

Regardless of where you go to pull off the feat, collecting a buck in velvet, because of the limited time and locales where one can be taken, makes it one of the rarest, not to mention coolest, trophies in any deer hunter's collection. ⓗ

Under Pressure

See more deer throughout the season by learning to keep hunter pressure to a minimum.

"I could kill deer like that, too, if I were hunting inside a high fence." The middle-aged hunter's voice carried with it an air of accusation as he glared at the TV screen, on which an outdoor show host gloated over a buck he had just arrowed.

While no doubt there are some shows filmed inside high-fence hunt operations, I knew this show host, and I knew the place he was hunting. It was no high fence. I had heard such accusations countless times before from hunters with whom I'd shared camp or a conversation, and while I understood some of the jealousy and distrust of watching somebody with apparent privilege, this guy's assessment was unfounded. It would have been more accurate to say that the show host was hunting at a top-shelf operation, one managed to minimize hunter pressure, which translated to more shot opportunities at quality deer.

I have come to believe that the single biggest factor that affects deer habits and movement is hunter pressure. Minimize it, and you can enjoy seeing deer nearly every time you climb in a stand. Amplify it, and you are virtually guaranteed to see little to nothing just days into a season.

Never hunt a stand if the wind isn't right, and don't overhunt it either. Give it plenty of rest between visits so as not to pressure deer in the area.

WALK SOFTLY

About eight or nine years ago, the small group of guys I hunt with started to get serious about managing the deer on our farm. The effort began with the decision to let the smaller bucks walk, but it soon expanded to not only wanting to increase the quality of our bucks, but also the quality of our hunting experience. That meant mitigating evidence of our presence in the woods so that deer would feel comfortable moving about.

Weeks prior to opening day and throughout the season, we no longer allow the driving of trucks around the property. Where hunters once drove to the backs of fields or down lanes to get as close to their stand as possible, they now walk from the house. The only exceptions: electric golf carts or utility vehicles such as the Stealth, which I recently tested.

We used to do drives during midday throughout the season, but now we reserve those for the final week in order to limit activity as well. The result has been dramatic. When our neighbors use their trucks and run all over the properties around us, the activity pushes deer onto our place, where we are spotting them more throughout the season.

In addition, treat your entire hunting time as if it were archery season by wearing rubber boots and spraying down with scent-eliminating sprays such as Code Blue EliminX or Primos Silver XP. Don't bust through areas where deer might be bedded; rather, take the quietest and most direct trail to your stands both in and out every time. When walking with a hunting partner, keep voices low and talking to a minimum. The sound of talking carries much farther than people sometimes realize, particularly in the early morning and late evening when the air is cool and dense.

DON'T FORCE IT

A lot of guys decide they want to hunt a particular stand or food plot because a big buck has been seen in the area or large numbers of deer have been moving through, but no matter how much promise a stand might offer, never hunt it if the wind isn't right. Even when you are hunting with a rifle, your scent can be picked up by deer more than 100 yards away.

Go into an area where a big buck has been working, and if he winds you just once, he is apt to change his pattern or go nocturnal. Check the wind before you select your stand using a map to confirm the relationship of your hunting location to the area you will be watching. Always carry a wind checker, such as Hunter's Specialties' Windicator powder, to check wind periodically while in your stand and prevent having your presence betrayed by swirling breezes.

CREATE A SANCTUARY

Real Deal Taxidermy's David Sichik shoots hunting videos on the small properties common to his native New Jersey and has found success creating sanctuary areas on properties as small as 60 or 70 acres.

"I'll pick an area that has a lot of cover for bedding and protection and won't go into it all season," he says. Sanctuary areas as small as five acres can be effective in providing deer with the security they need to remain on a property, and they'll even gravitate there from neighboring tracts. On larger hunting lands, multiple sanctuary areas of 10 to 20 acres spread around the property and located near easily accessible food sources are even better. Resist the urge to enter these areas even as deer activity slows throughout the season. Instead, locate active deer trails that go in and out of the sanctuaries toward food plots or oak flats, and set stands along these travel corridors near the fringe of the protected area. Then you can catch deer moving in and out of them at first light or just before dark.

STAND FREQUENCY

One of the biggest quandaries many hunters face is the question of how many times in a row or how frequently a stand should be hunted. Some hunters and guides are of the school of thought that to minimize the effects of hunting pressure, you should never hunt a stand two times in a row.

"You have to give a spot rest because deer will quickly clue on to you going there," says Fred Law, deer hunting manager at Enon Plantation in Alabama. "Going there repeatedly lessens the odds of seeing the deer you want." Generally, Law and his guides won't put a hunter in a stand that has been hunted in the past four to five days. Enon's holdings are also large enough that the property has been divided into four tracts, each one rested after a group has hunted it until all four have gone through a rotation.

Aaron Volkmar of Tails of the Hunt in Iowa has a slightly different approach, particularly later in the season as deer focus their attention on remaining food sources.

"When deer are in an area, you have to hunt it. It's that simple," Volkmar says. He will put hunters on a stand or blind in the same area days in a row as long as they are seeing deer. To minimize the impact of their presence, he doesn't allow guides to drive them all the way to their stands and encourages all-day hunting in order to limit the amount of coming and going that can disturb deer.

The key is to simply limit your impact in a particular area. If you believe a stand will produce, hit it when it's right, and if you see deer moving but don't get a shot and want to return the next day, do so only if the wind conditions and your timing are such that you can get in and out without being detected. I would hesitate hunting it more than that without giving it a rest.

"Whether or not you realize it, your scent builds up in an area you have been sitting in, and each time you go in and out you rub [your scent] up against limbs and trees. The deer know you've been there," Law says. ●

How Much Does Size Matter?

Is our crazed obsession with giant bucks taking the fun out of hunting?

I heard the shot just before dark. The sound was so far off in the distance, I wasn't even sure it was one of our guys until I received the text confirming "buck down." I was elated. After three very cold and unproductive days of hunting Illinois' second gun season—in the famed Pike County, epicenter of big-buck hype, no less—not a man or woman among the 16 hunters in camp had fired a shot. A doe had slipped in behind me on that final evening of the hunt and busted me shifting in the stand, effectively ending my hunt with her alarmed blowing. As a result, I was left to the vicarious celebrations of another hunter's success.

The second text, received before I had even made it back to camp, was less reassuring. "Not sur buk is goin 2 B 140," it read. With a 140-inch minimum imposed upon the hunters by the outfitter, the apologies had already begun. I wondered how much my friend had possibly misjudged the buck that he shot and hoped he was wrong. Besides the typical ribbing—and sometimes truly critical judgment from other hunt-

When it comes to young bucks, most hunters agree: "Let them walk." When are they "trophy-sized"? When you think they are trophy-sized.

ers—shooting something undersized here also came with a potential financial penalty.

MY BAD

Back in camp, it was easy to find the truck with the deer in it, as everyone was gathered around the bed. The truth is, it was a darn nice buck. But it wasn't quite 140. Nevertheless, it was the largest deer the hunter from the Southeast had ever killed, still a reason for celebration. But as he accepted the congratulations from the weather-weary hunters, the look in his eyes betrayed the uncertainty he was feeling. Away from the rest of the group, he admitted disappointment in himself and his buck, saying maybe he shouldn't have pulled the trigger. It was the fourth hunt I had been on that fall where I had heard hunters apologizing for bucks they had shot.

The interesting thing about all of these "apology bucks" is that just 10 years ago, most of them would have been driven around the county on a tailgate to show them off, the lucky hunters telling their story again and again to anyone who cared to listen. I have to wonder if maybe the success of the quality deer management faithful and our own modern obsession with hunting giant bucks are beginning to warp our perspective. At the very least, maybe it is taking a little fun out of our sport. Don't get me wrong, I agree wholeheartedly with the principles of letting little bucks walk so they grow older and bigger. But I want to shoot sometimes, too! In the past few years, I probably haven't stood among a group of hunters gawking over a 140-inch or better bruiser on the meat pole where no matter how impressive the buck was, someone didn't say, "Imagine how big he would've been next year." So how big is big enough?

Can you compare deer from different parts of the country? It is probably a bad idea. What is considered a trophy in one place may still have a lot of growing to do in another.

KEEPING IT REAL

Obviously, the answer to that is that it depends. If hunting with an outfitter, it depends on the rules he has set to keep attracting clients and maintain a viable operation for years to come. Few hunters pay thousands of dollars for the chance to hunt does or little bucks. If hunting on privately owned or leased property, it depends on the owner or people in charge to decide what potential the land and herd hold in order to determine what a realistic minimum for the area is. I stress "realistic," because I think some older, more experienced or more determined hunters today are satisfied to hold out for years waiting on that monster buck to appear, while many others truthfully still want to pull the trigger or let arrows fly each season. Of course, if the owner says this is the minimum, regardless of what you think, you better follow the rules if you hope to get invited back. Many hunters will hold out for a while on their own land, but at some point, it's time to shoot. Then there remains the "if it's brown, it's down" faith-

BE HONEST WITH YOURSELF

It's one thing to make an honest mistake in judging deer size when hunting your own land or the land of a club or shared lease where you hunt. It can be quite another to make that mistake on a booked hunt where the outfitter may charge you anywhere from $500 to $1,500 extra for shooting an undersized animal. When booking a hunt or hunting as a guest where the herd is managed, ask up front what type of deer is permitted to be taken, and if necessary, ask for comparisons, such as a mounted deer on a wall, to make sure you are clear on what is big enough. When it comes to age, that gets a little trickier for some hunters, but QDMA sells resources on its Web site (qdma.com) that can help you out.

If you are not comfortable with your ability to judge and meet the minimum standards or are not willing to hold out for such a minimum, look elsewhere; this isn't the hunting spot for you. There are plenty of outfitters who will encourage you to take a certain size deer, but permit a guy to take one that he is happy with regardless of antler size. Whether you are paying money or simply hunting locally with friends, in the end, hunting should be fun. If you are going to have to worry with every deer you see whether or not to shoot, then educate yourself by getting out as often as possible or choose a hunt where a guide sits with you and can help be the decision maker on when to shoot.

ful, a diminishing lot in today's world, which is an evolution most modern sportsmen will agree is a good thing.

To get a better perspective, I went to the head of the Quality Deer Management Association himself, Brian Murphy.

"We've talked about this very thing here at QDMA," he says. "The proliferation of magazines and television shows that focus on hunting big whitetails makes it look like if hunters don't shoot a super-big buck, they are somehow less of a hunter. But if you hunt fair chase on land that you manage and the buck is nice for where you hunt, you should be proud."

That is particularly true when comparing bucks—or hunters, for that matter—in different parts of the country.

"You can't compare a buck killed in South Carolina to one shot in Illinois," Murphy says. "If a hunter kills a 105-inch buck in Florida, it is a heck of an accomplishment."

Rather than focusing on antlers, Murphy suggests that the true mark of a trophy deer and the effort it takes to successfully hunt it is based on age.

"That's the real measure of a trophy. If you are killing bucks in the top 10 percent of the age bracket for your area, you are doing great," says the QDMA leader. "Killing a five-year-old in Alabama when compared to killing a three-year-old in Illinois can be much more impressive even though that three-year-old's rack will likely be larger than the buck from Alabama.

"I hope the benchmark will ultimately become buck age rather than antlers."

WHAT'S IN A TROPHY?

There are, of course, other factors that can play into the trophy aspect of a hunt that often get lost in the excitement over big antlers. It might be the strategy a hunter used, the novelty of the bow or gun he shot, even the circumstances of the hunt. It might be an unusually spectacular shot that was made, where the hunt took place or even the person with whom the hunt was shared.

Even where age is concerned, Murphy concedes that while today's hunters have become much more skilled at aging deer on the hoof and sizing up antlers in the field, there are still plenty of hunters who haven't and maybe don't even care to. Regardless, Murphy says, in the end, hunting should still always be a good time, not one that causes worry.

"Keep it fun. If you can shoot deer that are in the top 10 percent of your neighborhood, you are doing as good as anybody can expect," he says. "Every hunter is going to make a mistake at some point and shoot an antlered buck that is a little smaller than he meant to take or mistake a button buck for a doe. As long as he is genuinely trying to adhere to the management plan, he may still deserve a little ribbing in good fun, but nobody should be mad or angry about it.

"Accidentally killing a small buck or two or a few button bucks off of a property isn't going to set your management plan back. Deer are a renewable resource; there will be more of them. Now, if a hunter does it several times in a season or year after year, OK, then somebody needs to have a talk with him." Sounds sensible to me. ⊞

Plot Your Success

Late-summer food plots give your coming deer season its best chance.

August is a time of both excitement and concern. Excitement because in little more than a month, many bow seasons are going to open, providing a crack at the coming autumn's first bucks (and if you hunt South Carolina's Lowcountry, gun season opens mid-heat wave). Concern because inevitably there is a list of projects as long as my arm that need to be done on the properties I hunt.

Sure, I could just wing it and accept that deer will be on the land as they always are and hope I'm in the right spot when one walks by, but I like to narrow the odds as much as possible. The single best thing any hunter can do to put those odds in his favor come opening day is to plant something deer will want to eat or identify key food sources that will naturally draw deer. Best of all, it doesn't have to take a ton of time or money.

LOCATION, LOCATION, LOCATION

Grab a recent satellite image of the land you're hunting, and identify four key areas: good cover, existing openings, existing food sources such as planted crop fields and oak stands, and, of course, areas where you've traditionally seen a lot of deer. After you've marked these spots on the map, highlight the ones that are toward the interior of your property and away from roads. You

Timing is critical when planting plots preseason to create peak attraction when it counts.

also don't want interference from hunters on adjoining properties.

The closer to a bedding area and the less human traffic a spot receives, the more likely it is going to produce throughout the season. Hopefully, you have some existing trails, log decks and even old openings or slightly neglected fields that can easily be mowed, disked and planted without having to clear timber.

These highlighted spots are the ones you want to plant. Don't waste time or money planting spots that will be disturbed by others outside your group of hunters.

TAKE A SHOTGUN APPROACH

It would be great if all of us owned huge fields and had the equipment and resources to plant them in clover and brassicas, but that's not reality for most of us. Seed and fertilizer can get expensive fast, so identify how much acreage you have to plant, how much you can afford to plant, then spread out some of your plantings across the interior of your property in areas close to good bedding areas where deer can slip in and out with minimal travel once the guns start booming. That's a better option than just planting one big, impressive field and sitting the same area every time you hunt.

"For a guy with about four acres available to plant, I would highly recommend, if he is working with a set budget, to do one or two acres and do it right rather

WHAT TO PLANT

Manufacturers have responded by making some great annual mixes designed specifically to grow fast in late summer and early fall with minimal care. Most hunters think clover, and while it is good to toss some of the perennial in with whatever you decide to plant, clover works best in loamy soils and won't establish much benefit when planted in the fall. It will, however, establish roots, go dormant in the cold and jump-start any spring planting you might be considering.

Top planting options for fall include winter wheat, oats, rye and brassicas. Some of my favorite mixes I've had luck with on my property include Whitetail Institute's Pure Attraction, a mix of forage oats, winter peas and brassicas that sprout early for the rut but provide food throughout the colder months as well, and their Tall Tine Tubers, a mix of brassicas and turnips that will sweeten upon the first big frost and deer will relish. I've also enjoyed great success with Hunter's Specialties' Vita-Rack E-Z Grow, Vita-Rack Winter Forage and Biologic's Full Draw. Winter peas from a local feed-and-seed store also do great and quite often are extremely affordable.

If the land you hunt has crop fields planted in soybeans, corn or wheat that will be harvested and wiped out by late fall, focus early-season hunts on those spots. That's where the deer will be, barring the dropping of white oak acorns. Plant all of your plots with late-season brassicas so you can transition to these new spots with cold weather. If you hunt somewhere as nutritionally barren as a Southern pine plantation, be darn sure you plant a mix that will produce early so you attract deer and get the first crack at the biggest feeding bucks with a bow before the gun boys roll in later in the season.

For the hunter looking to establish small spots with minimal effort, Whitetail Institute's No Plow and Secret Spot mixes, as well as Evolved Habitat's Throw & Gro, both require little more than raking out an area, roughing up the dirt and hand broadcasting fertilizer and seed. It gets no easier than that and can make more of a difference in your hunting success than buying that new gun or scope. Ⓗ

than spread it out over four acres and do everything haphazard," says Whitetail Institute's Steve Scott. That means locating four or five smaller open areas to disk and plant.

THE RIGHT SIZE

When selecting spots to be planted, ideally you want them a half acre to one acre in size, though plots as small as 1/3 of an acre can work really well, particularly when tucked away among heavy cover that has limited natural forage. Smaller than that and deer can over-browse the plot before hunting season ever arrives. Try to plant areas that have a north-south orientation rather than an east-west one so that the sun travels across the width of the area throughout the remaining growing season, but won't bake the soil dry in those late-summer/early-autumn days where the mercury still soars.

The Bucks Of Summer

Be the first hunter on your lease to join the big-buck contest.

My college roommate Danny Rollins was a lot like a big ol' nasty buck. At the very least, he could be patterned like one in the early season when much of the focus is on food. Early in the evening, Danny was either at a friend's house scoring on his cheap beer and whatever food he could scavenge or hitting the bar with the best happy hour deal—particularly one that included grub. I knew exactly where he would be by the advertised bar specials of the week. To a whitetail, that part of Danny's evening would equal early season when the bucks are still hanging together in groups and more focused on filling their stomachs. For the deer hunter looking to start his season right, there are more than a few lessons Danny's life can teach them.

With bow seasons opening up very soon in many states, take a lesson from Danny's early-evening ritual and focus on food. But don't plop down in a stand alongside a big field. Do that and you'll see deer, but you're less likely to actually connect on one. First identify which food sources bucks are hitting, then determine exactly how they are accessing them. With a bow, setting your stand just 10 yards too far from where a buck walks can mean the difference between filling a tag and never getting a shot.

A heavy acorn crop will keep bucks in the cover of the forest and out of the fields even when they hold prime soybeans or corn.

WORKING FIELDS

Before hunting a crop field, spend a few evenings glassing when and where a bruiser enters to feed. Hopefully, you've identified a couple of likely spots to scout out with the help of trail cameras prior to the season. Deer shouldn't be pressured yet, so providing that the weather and wind remain consistent, bucks should show up in the same spot most afternoons. After pinpointing from which trail a nice buck enters the field, slip in early one afternoon and set up within 20 yards downwind of the spot. Try to keep the sun at your back.

With pressure light and the weather still fairly hot, if there is ample cover near the field, be careful about venturing too far into the woods. Deer are apt to bed close, and walking in will just blow them out of the area. Never walk down the edge of a field to access a stand. Go through the middle, where if deer step out and begin browsing the edge, they are less likely to cut your scent trail and spook before they've had a chance to filter your way.

MAST IS THE MAINSTAY

When white oak acorns are dropping, little else matters to whitetails. These acorns are among the most preferred whitetail foods in the forest. Check wide-topped white oaks before the season to identify whether acorns are

EARLY-SEASON OPTICS

Binoculars, even for bowhunters, are a critical piece of gear. Every hunter needs a decent set whether it's for scouting before and during the season, sizing up a buck in low light or just seeing what came out of the woods at the other end of the field to determine if that is where you need to set up next time. Go with something like Nikon's Monarch X ATB binocular. It's a good midsize 45mm objective binocular with great clarity and light transmission. It can be had for less than $600 and in some places much less. Regardless of which brand you buy, get a 10X or 10.5X instead of the lower 8X. The extra magnification only helps, and cost-wise, the difference is rarely more than $20 or $40. —*DH*

---

expansive pine plantations in the South, focus on natural browse that deer will seek out for food. The wild greens shooting up throughout these otherwise nutritionally barren forests can provide a succulent feast for whitetails, but you have to know where to look. Because most green stuff looks the same to the average hunter, you can spend your time with a *Petersen's Field Guide to Plants* or you can go where plants are going to shoot up with the most verve and nutritional value. That would be in a first-year clear cut or recent burn.

In the former, ample sunlight allows new plants to grow quickly and produce more nutrition. In the latter, the fires that clear the understory also regenerate the nutrients in the soil, giving rise to heady growth. Find these spots bordering areas that provide ample cover and you have yourself a jackpot of possibilities. It's kind of like that grilled cheese sandwich when there is no pizza to be had—it sounds pretty good. Likewise, if you know where natural fruits such as wild scuppernong or muscadine grapes are growing, or, even better, persimmon or old apple and pear trees from a former orchard, set up on those once the fruits begin to ripen. Deer will be on those like my friend on a free beer.

HAPPY HOUR

Last, remember that, like man—and my buddy Danny—deer do not live on food alone. They require liquid refreshment, and when it's blazing outside, fair amounts of it. In a whitetail's case that translates into water. Seek out isolated ponds or water holes that may provide the only water in an area, or look for abundant tracks along creek banks and swamp edges where deer are crossing and/or catching a sip. Deer will move in the cool of the shade along these natural traffic corridors and drink up before heading out to eat in the evening. Think of it as happy hour for deer. Set up along a beaver dam (deer will often walk across that rather than swim deep water), a shallow crossing or a track-pocked pond edge and it could well be happy hour for you as well. ⓑ

---

present. Sometimes only a few oaks will be laden with the tasty nuts, so don't just set up under the same oak you've always hunted.

Monitor when acorns begin to drop, and when they do, that's where you need to be. Even if Farmer John just cut his corn field and littered the ground with waste grain or the soybeans are lush and green, the cover of the forest and the protein in the acorns will keep bucks hidden from sight unless you're there to watch. Think about it: If I called Danny to tell him I was making grilled cheese sandwiches and then someone else invited him over for pizza, where do you think he'd go?

NATURAL BROWSE

If you hunt an area that is devoid of fields or any sizeable food plots, particularly areas such as the

---

The Ultimate Whitetail Decoy

Combine a decoy with a full-body mount for the ultimate in tricking bucks this fall.

I am infatuated with hunting decoys. Something about pulling the wool over my quarry's eyes just tickles the heck out of me: "Ha, ha, I tricked you!" It's often a childlike amusement, but when a mature, rut-crazed whitetail locks in on your decoy, then comes looking to kick some serious ass, it's a heart-pounding bowhunting experience that is highly addictive. Whitetail hunting doesn't get any better.

My first hunting decoy was home-made. It was an antelope silhouette I made out of cardboard. Next I started chopping turkey decoys into pieces to create my own versions. I made one strutter with a moveable fan (similar to Primos' Killer B decoy) that I used to ruin many a gobbler's day. Over the years, my desire for more and more realistic-looking decoys has become an obsession. I don't want to fool just some critters, I want to fool all of them.

In 2008 I traveled on a whitetail hunt with my good friend Bill Pellegrino. Just prior to that hunt, Bill had his taxidermist build a full-body doe mount, reinforced with rebar so it could be used as a decoy. He then had it fitted with a removable set of antlers and placed on an aluminum base so it could be firmly planted in the ground. When I first saw Bill's new decoy, I thought it looked great, but I worried that the hair would retain odors that might alert deer as they approached. I was wrong. I saw it in action and was amazed. It drew deer like flies, and Bill killed a stud of a buck over it that year.

The quest for the ultimate whitetail decoy may have ended.

Photo Credit: Bill Jackson

After that trip I had to have one, only I wanted mine to be even better; I wanted to build the ultimate whitetail decoy. The only concerns I had about Bill's decoy were that it was very heavy and I wasn't sure how it would hold up to an all-out buck attack. Although his decoy was reinforced to some degree, the foam forms used by taxidermists are not intended to take such abuse. Antlers could certainly penetrate the hide-covered foam and possibly rip it in half or, even worse, run off with it.

I use a great taxidermist named Don Fager, and together we came up with a few ideas. First, rather than using a foam taxidermy form, we decided to mount a whitetail doe cape on an actual Carry-Lite deer decoy. The Carry-Lite has a very realistic shape and provides a lightweight, impenetrable core that's proven time and again that it's up to the challenge of being beaten down by angry bucks. Heck, that decoy works great as it is, but I was going for the ultimate.

I took my Carry-Lite to Don, and he got started. Neither of us was sure how it would look once the doe cape was fitted, but after making a few adjustments, we discovered that the realistically shaped Carry-Lite makes a pretty awesome taxidermy form. Don fit the decoy with a removable set of whitetail sheds so it could be used as either a buck or a doe, but the back end of this decoy is what really sets it apart. Don installed a tail unit that we borrowed from another decoy called the

Easy Doe, which utilizes a remote-controlled motor to flick the tail from side to side. It is a very realistic movement that is capable of catching a buck's attention from great distances. Some states, however, do not allow the use of electronics in decoys. Simply pulling the batteries out of the tail unit quickly nullifies such issues. Even without the tail movement I knew this decoy would be deadly, but with it, it's truly the ultimate.

Every great decoy must have a name, and I decided to name mine after the man who built it. When using it as a buck, I call my decoy Don. Then with the antlers removed, I simply lengthen it to Donna.

To say I was anxious to put my new ultimate whitetail decoy to the test is an understatement. By the time November arrived I was foaming at the mouth. Finally, I was off to Iowa, the land of giants. When I arrived, I met up with my buddy who first inspired me, Bill Pellegrino. The day before I arrived, Bill had killed another dandy buck over his decoy. He explained that the bucks were really searching for does and he was having better luck with his decoy by leaving off the antlers.

I used Donna for the next three days, and the action was incredible. What a show! If you have ever used a whitetail decoy, you probably know how whitetail does usually react to them. They typically hate them, stomping and blowing before breaking hell-bent for cover. Well, they didn't react that way to Donna. Does and bucks alike fell in love with her. One young buck strolled right up and proceeded to take advantage of her for at least a half hour, mounting her time and time again until he finally knocked her over. Even then, he didn't spook. He eventually wandered off, no doubt in awe of his own masculine prowess and the effect it seemed to have on poor ol' Donna.

On my third afternoon I set Donna out in a long, narrow wheat field that was shaped much like a golf club. I positioned her right at the base of where the handle would meet the club head so she could be seen from both ends. The field separated two major bedding areas, and I was confident that bucks would be crossing it as they checked each area for hot does. It worked out just as I planned. First a young buck came charging down the narrow handle end of the field toward Donna. Just as he started to get comfortable with her, I heard several loud grunts from where the young buck had just come. When the youngster bolted, I knew there was a good chance that the bully coming in would be a shooter. When he appeared, every hair on his back was standing at full attention. He looked as if he were half gorilla.

Taxidermist Don Fager, hard at work on Danny's full-body mount decoy, aptly named Don or Donna depending upon tranny getup.

All the anger and testosterone was more than this bowhunter could take. I drew my bow at the first opportunity and then watched a Lumenok-lit arrow fly through the big buck's lungs.

Decoying whitetails during the rut is by far my favorite way to hunt them. Nothing is more exciting than fooling a rut-crazed buck like that bully from Iowa. But for a tinkerer like me, using a custom decoy of my own design, well, it's added yet another dimension. To me, it's simply the ultimate.

Authors Note: If you are interested in having Don build you a custom decoy of your own, contact him at (719) 495-3868 or visit him on the Web at —donstaxidermy.net Ⓗ

Using decoys under the right situations **WORKS.**

Ultimate Deer Surveillance

Used strategically, trail cameras will deliver the intel you need in order to know where and when to tag your next trophy.

In a business where virtually every new product is overhyped as the greatest thing to help you see and kill more animals, trail cameras for deer hunters truly live up to the hype. In fact, many hunters have yet to get the most performance from their cameras, using them to snap photos of big bucks and little else.

"Trail cameras are being used a lot more as a beauty pageant," says NorthCountry Whitetails co-owner and wildlife consultant Neil Dougherty. "[Hunters] look at how nice this buck is and that buck is." Today's trail cams include a range of infrared triggering sensors, image formats and other features that can ultimately not only reveal what size deer are roaming a property, but actually help a hunter decipher when and where he should hunt in order to nail one of those monsters. But you have to know how to strategically set them up to pull this off.

PROPER SETUP

Many hunters take whatever cameras they have before the season—whether it is one or a dozen—and hang them next to bait sites or feeders where deer will congregate. This is great for nailing down a rough census

Location, location: Hang cameras no more than three feet off the ground, and aim them north or south to avoid the sun's glare in the morning or evening.

of how many deer are in a particular area and if any big bucks are around, but there is more that can be done to enhance your scouting efforts.

To start, hang cameras no more than three feet off the ground to ensure that sensors hit passing deer at center of mass, where core body temperatures, body motion and mass will better trigger cameras. Aim them north or south to avoid the sun's glare in the morning or evening and ensure clear images at times when deer are most apt to move. A camera aimed toward the rising or setting sun also increases the amount of shadows from limbs or brush, which will trigger false images from sensors tripped by the sudden temperature change. If you are getting a lot of images with nothing but scenery, this may be your problem.

Moultrie's Mike Mattly recommends hanging cameras just inside the timber instead of on the edges. This will catch more bucks traveling through an area, since they are more comfortable moving in cover, and hang them facing down trails as well instead of perpendicular to them, where they will only catch animals quickly passing by.

Hunters using corn or other food attractants can get more mileage out of their bait by including scents or a taste that works itself into the soil, explains Major Person (yeah, that's really his name) with Wildgame Innovations. The company's Acorn Rage and Sugarbeet Crush are scented attractants that soak into the soil and keep deer coming back even after food has been eaten.

"When corn is gone, it is gone, but scent soaks into the soil and the deer will keep hitting it until you can get back out there," Person says.

Products such as Primos Swamp Donkey or Hunter's Specialties Vita-Rack 26 Lick Site are inexpensive attractants that can be poured onto the soil and used to establish a location that deer will return to long after the attractant has been consumed or washed into the ground. But don't get so hung up on bait sites that you only focus your surveillance efforts on them. As the season draws near, usually about mid-September, move cameras over scrapes—either real or mock—and along pinch points in travel corridors such as in a point of woods or an opening in a fence. This will help you identify key stand sites to hunt as bucks begin to transition from summer feeding to autumn rut patterns.

HOW MANY CAMS?

This is a tricky question to answer simply because every hunter's hunting land and budget are different. Mattly personally likes to hang one camera for every 40 acres of land. Dougherty will stretch his out a little farther, shooting for one cam per 80 to 100 acres. The bottom line is, if you can only afford one camera, then at least get one. Whether hunting 50 acres or 500, I strongly recommend buying at

Scents/attractants work into the soil to keep deer coming back.

least three or four. Several cameras allow you to simultaneously monitor alternate spots. This gives you an idea of where to hunt at a given time. While hunting one location, your other cams can monitor different spots. If you can't monitor 12 different locations, so what. Most guys aren't going to hunt that many in a week's or even a season's time anyway. Many of us have our favorite spots identified and will hunt them until we feel it's time to move on. A trail cam can help make that decision with confidence.

KEY CAM FUNCTIONS

Many of today's cams give the user the option to choose whether he wants to shoot still images or capture video, while some models, such as Moultrie's M-100 and M-80 mini cams, even include a time-lapse

mode that snaps images or video at regular intervals. Here are some thoughts on each of these:

Video—The ability to record video is nice, and a lot of guys are going to want a camera that can do this. The reality, however, is that once most hunters capture a few cool videos on their cams, they will switch back to images. Why?

"Video is a neat feature, but what everybody is really looking for is a good photo of that buck," says Mattly. "You will always get more sightings of does and fawns than big bucks, and it is quicker to view single images than wait for a video to play where you can see whether a buck was filmed." Video also takes up more space on your SD card and drains batteries more quickly.

REMOTE SURVEILLANCE

I've been a huge fan of my SmartScouter for years. It snaps shots of deer and e-mails them to a Web site where I can log on and view them from anywhere I can access the Internet. It even e-mails me when new images have been uploaded, allowing me to get real-time intel on what is in a given spot and when. Wireless camera technology pioneer BuckEye Cam is awesome as well, as it allows you to set up as many as 30 cameras and transmit images to a single computer base that you control, creating the ultimate whitetail surveillance network. Of course, none of these options is cheap.

For the more budget-conscious sportsman looking to gain remote surveillance ability without all the cost, Wildgame Innovations Pulse cameras sell for less than $200, and when combined with the YN1 WiFi Module, each camera can send out a WiFi signal that will allow you to access camera data from as far as 300 feet away with a computer or smart tablet. There is no monthly cost for a cell service plan, and while you won't be able to check data from anywhere in the world, it does allow you to check images without stinking up the spot with human scent. *—DH*

Triggered Still Images—This is the meat and potatoes of what every good camera must deliver. Hunters want to catch solid snapshots of bucks they can study and examine, and only pictures do this. By setting a camera to capture only motion- or temperature-change-triggered images, you save on both battery life and card space, allowing your camera to work as long as it needs to. A still camera with good trigger speed trumps video ability every time in my book.

Time-Lapse Images—Cameras such as the Day 6 PlotWatcher or Moultrie's Plot Stalker, M-100 and M-80 cameras can snap images at regular intervals on a plot or field. On Moultrie's models you can snap images from every 15 seconds (for 3,600 images a day) to once an hour and any interval in between. This allows you to monitor an entire field throughout the day and even night, determining when and exactly where deer are entering to feed—even if they are too far away to trigger the camera.

"I have a couple of big plots where I knew bucks were coming to feed, but I had no clue where. Using a camera in Plot Stalker mode fixed that problem," Mattly says. A camera that combines both triggered and time-lapse images may well be the way to go, and with growing awareness of the latter feature, more models in the future are likely to include that ability. Ⓗ

Backpack Your Buck

Using your feet to retrieve your precious meat.

For big-game hunters, the greatest challenge of taking their pursuits far from the car isn't the hike. It's an age-old question. If I shoot something back here, how in the heck will I get it out?

In my circle of acquaintances, that issue has cost a number of folks more than a few trophy animals. One friend, hunting the uplands of the Bridger Mountains near Bozeman, Montana, agonized over pulling the trigger on a tremendous mule deer for the better part of a half-hour. He finally turned his tired boots back down the mountain. A few years ago, while hunting elk in the backcountry south of Jackson, Wyoming, I lowered the hammer on my .444 Marlin with a bull elk whose main beams extended handily behind his front shoulders. A seven-mile trek back to the trailhead in unfamiliar territory after dark dissuaded the shot. In hindsight, I wish I'd stuck a Hornady flat-point through the elk's front shoulder and holed up with the carcass overnight.

For many hunters, regretting such a decision isn't even in the realm of possibility. If you don't know how to efficiently retrieve a big buck or bull from the backcountry, you're certainly not going to shoot it. However, it's really not that difficult to bring the meat (and antlers) of an animal from the outback to civilization. All you need is a sturdy backpack, a sharp knife and an understanding of where to cut.

Choosing a backpack to carry meat confronts the hunter with a bewildering array of options. While it's tempting to opt for a large-capacity pack, unless you're actually hunting from a backpack camp where you're ferrying camping gear, I'm not keen on high-capacity packs. With boneless meat, weight becomes an issue long before space. Most reasonably fit hunters can tolerate a load in the 35- to 50-pound range. Fit, strong individuals accustomed to heavy loads might add another 10 to 20 pounds. I once carried an 80-pound pack with the meat from a mountain goat and its head and cape down a mountain for a mile and have moved a similar load of whitetail buck uphill for about the same distance. However, carrying a 35- to 50-pound load is much more realistic, especially in difficult terrain over a span of several miles.

With those figures in mind, let's start by noting you'll add at least 10 pounds with the weight of your pack, water, snacks and other gear. This leaves around 25 to 40 pounds for meat. To lend a more scientific perspective, I recently weighed a load of meat in relation to its volume from a whitetail buck my son killed in the Beartooth Mountains. We boned the animal and packed it about two miles, an easy undertaking with a young buck and two fit hunters. We found a 35-pound load of meat (not counting pack weight and other gear) required a little over 1,000 cubic inches (ci). Based simply on volume, a medium-sized daypack will enclose more meat than the average hunter wants to carry.

Given the high weight-to-volume ratio of game meat, my favorite type of hunting pack is a medium-capacity (around 3,000 ci), internal frame pack. A pack of this nature is compact and light enough to carry all day as a daypack. If you kill a buck, there's room to pack a load of meat on the way out.

Packs of this size come from two types of manufacturers: those who make "hunting" packs and

With a bit of knowledge and effort, most will enjoy the rewarding act of game retrieval.

those who produce backpacks with no specific intention for hunting. Both types have pros and cons. "Hunting" packs are most often created from "quiet" fabric and have some specific design elements for hunting, such as straps for securing a rifle or a binocular pocket. However, they're often heavier than standard backpacks and overengineered with too many accoutrements that add unnecessary weight and are only nominally useful. Backpacks from mid to high-end backpack manufacturers tend to be lighter than "hunting" packs. Overall, I

think they're also more comfortable. On the downside, they're usually made from material that's noisy when pushing through brush and may not lend themselves to carrying a rifle on the pack.

This fall, my son and I utilized three different backpacks from various manufacturers for packing meat. The first was a Badlands 2200 (badlandspacks.com). A hunting pack advertised at a 2,300 ci capacity, the 2200 has an actual volume of around 2,700 ci. Its camo-colored shell is composed of soft, quiet material. Although the advertised weight is 6 pounds, 4 ounces, the 2200 I used weighed exactly 6 pounds out of the box. This Badlands pack carries comfortably loaded with meat but has a bit of a bulky feel. An integrated pouch that zips away when not in use cradles the butt of a rifle stock, allowing the user to carry a rifle, balanced in the middle of the pack, secured with two straps. There are a lot of pockets and pouches on the 2200, probably a few too many for those with a minimalist bent. Nonetheless, this is a rugged, functional pack for folks who don't mind a bit of extra weight and bulk. The 2200 sells for $260 from Cabela's.

On the other side of the spectrum were two packs from traditional backpacking companies: Coleman and Mountainsmith. The Coleman Traipse X45 (coleman.com) is a budget-minded internal-frame pack with a 2,750 ci capacity. It consists of a large main compartment with a smaller top compartment on the "lid" and another outer pocket, good for stashing clothes or gloves. A rifle can be carried by placing the butt in one of the water bottle pockets and lashing down the compression straps above the pocket. The advertised weight of 3.02 pounds was within ounces of the tested pack. My son used this lightweight pack for carrying meat this fall with satisfactory results on approximately a 35-pound load. At this writing, the price for the X45 on Coleman's website is $75.

My personal favorite among backpacks with meat-handling capacity has to be the Mountainsmith Lookout 45 (mountainsmith.com). This is not a hunting pack per se, but doubles very well as a daypack and meat pack. The Lookout 45 has a 2,870 ci capacity that extends to 3,235. Its main compartment has a useful, removable divider. There's a zippered map pocket under the lid and a couple of other nice-sized pockets for gear storage. Advertised and actual weights are 4 pounds, 2 ounces. I've handled 50 pounds of meat in this nimble pack comfortably, even though it's not technically marketed for heavy loads. A rifle carries easily via a water bottle pocket and side compression straps. Mountain-smith's web price is $160.

No matter what pack you choose, your back will thank you for minimizing the extraneous carcass weight brought from the backcountry. Quartering or completely deboning an animal is a weight-shedding and relatively simple job. As deboning is my preferred method (check your state regulations for evidence of sex and carcass retrieval requirements), here's the quick explanation of how to accomplish it.

With the animal on its side, make a dorsal cut along the spine from the tailbone to the base of the skull. Peel the skin away, from the backbone to the belly, exposing the front and hind quarters. Applying upward pressure to the leg, remove the front shoulder by severing the connective tissue in the animal's "armpit." Cut the meat from the front shoulder. Remove the hind quarter by severing the muscle from the bone along the pelvis. Continue the cut through the ball-and-socket joint, then completely detach the hind quarter by slicing the muscle away from the lower portion of the backbone. Cut the meat from the hind quarter by working your knife around the bones. Once you get the hang of it, the entire rear quarter can be deboned in a single piece. Strip the loin from the ribs and backbone. Taking care not to puncture the paunch, open the body cavity behind the ribs and peel out the tenderloin. Flip the animal over and repeat the process. Trim the neck meat and other pieces from the carcass for grinding. Place the boned meat in game bags (one bag for each half of a deer).

Over the last decade, I've backpacked dozens of deer and elk from the backcountry using this method. It's a great way to stay fit, engenders a strong sense of self-reliance and, best of all, allows me to prowl remote swatches of habitat where bucks and bulls get big. Ⓗ

Under Pressure

Here's how to use it—and lose it—to your advantage.

This past season opened with the highest optimism yet among my hunting group. Deer were flocking to our food plots, and trail cams had snapped photos of of trophy-sized bucks. And the simple fact that we had been passing on smaller bucks for years should've translated into more wallhangers tromping about the land.

By season's close, we'd taken three decent bucks and a handful of does. Analyzing our success, however, most of the guys felt the year hadn't measured up. Few had seen a shooter buck. Others hadn't taken any does. On the other hand, I had passed up several bucks that matched the size of the one I tagged opening day, spotted several gaggers out of range and saw deer nearly every time I sat on a stand. I was dismissed as "lucky," which in any hunting is always a little true. But there are ways to improve your luck and see more deer. First, you have to analyze why deer movement is stagnant. As is virtually always the case, it comes down to hunting pressure.

The author found success this season by focusing on stand locations far from where his fellow hunters were setting up on a regular basis.

PRESSURE POINTS

"Bottom line, bucks and does are conditioned to avoiding threats," says Grant Woods, one of the leading land management and hunting consultants in the country.

"It's a conditioned response, so as soon as a situation arises that makes a deer feel threatened, they're going to alter their patterns. For hunters to be successful, they have to get outside of that conditioned response."

Woods was involved in a project where a group of hunters were brought in to manage the deer herd on 11,000 acres that hadn't been hunted in a decade.

"Deer were everywhere, and they made no effort to run away when they saw a hunter because they did not associate humans with danger," says Woods. The first three years, the group shot only does. By the end of that time, a hunter was hard pressed to see a doe. They fled as soon as a man was spotted. Bucks, even mature ones, still milled in the open throughout the day. Does had responded to the pressure by equating humans to danger, while the bucks remained unfazed. So what does this mean for the hunter who wants to see deer all season long? He has to minimize pressure, or he has to focus his hunting efforts outside those spots where whitetails feel threatened. Or better, do both.

PRESSURE RELIEF

Do everything to limit noise, smell and activity on your property. Don't drive trucks through hunting land, unless they are driven there year round. Where tractors and farmers regularly come and go or where trucks checking oil or gas operations frequently pass, the effect a vehicle will have on deer will be minimal. But if that's not the case, walk or use an electric cart that makes little noise. Avoid ATV use. Unless they are absolutely needed for retrieval, stay off of them or park them far from where you hunt. ATVs are an awesome tool that many hunters depend on, but they are loud and spook deer.

Don't sight-in firearms the day before the season unless people regularly shoot there year round. Woods has watched deer feed within sight of a shooting range, because they were never shot at there and were used to the sound. That's not the case in most places. Sight-in rifles well before the season or use a range far from your hunting land.

When walking to stands, don't talk on your cell phone or to hunting partners walking with you. Strap stands and other equipment together tightly to avoid rattling. Spray down with a scent-free spray before you leave and be cautious about the wind as you approach a stand.

"A lot of hunters choose a stand that has good wind, but forget how that wind is blowing as they approach the stand," says Woods. "I don't want to lose that deer and blow him out of the area before I get into my stand."

While the economics of land leasing and ownership make hunting public land or sharing a place with multiple hunters the only option for many, the fact remains the fewer hunters, the fewer disturbances there will be. Restrictive guest policies and limited members in a lease might be a social pain, but they'll improve your hunting if everyone works together to hunt with a low-impact approach.

OUTSIDE THE PRESSURE ZONE

Even with all of these efforts, deer will sense danger and alter their habits. Again, Woods stresses, hunters have to get outside a deer's conditioned response to threats.

On my farm this season, a pattern quickly emerged. The hunters all headed to spots where deer were seen before the season, and deer began avoiding these spots. Trail cams on food plots caught deer showing up right after shooting light, likely staging nearby. Using satellite images of the land, I identified bedding areas and likely travel routes or staging areas. I then selected unhunted spots and hit them with my climbing stand or sat on the ground only when the wind was right. I saw deer nearly every time. As my fellow hunters roamed, I tracked the spots getting hit and almost always hunted elsewhere.

It's critical to identify spots that are never hunted on a property, as that's likely where a big buck will hide. Patches of woods adjacent to a highway, cover behind a home or newly fallen trees with treetops providing tangled cover all offer spots worth setting up on. Also, getting outside of a deer's conditioned response is not just about place. It might be about time.

"It might mean hunting in the middle of the day instead of mornings and evenings," says Woods. "You won't see a deer every time, but it just takes that one time to hit it right." Ⓗ

QUICK STRIKE

Perhaps no tool is better for a hunter looking to change setups quickly and slide in and out of a spot as quietly as possible as a lightweight, well-configured climbing stand. We use them extensively in the Southeast where there are generally ample trees with tall straight trunks to allow a hunter to hit a spot when conditions are right, and if he doesn't score, be gone before deer are the wiser. Climbers work great in plenty of other wooded locals throughout the whitetail range.

Perhaps no company leads the way in climbing stands more than Summit Treestands (summitstands.com). I use a Blade model based off the popular Viper series, while the rest of my hunting crew use the Viper SD, which is basically an updated version of the original classic. This year, Summit has introduced two new variations, both with rounded aluminum tubing that reduces their weight another 20 percent. The Viper Elite SD is a 16-pound, closed-front climber perfect for gun hunters who can use the front as a rest; the Viper Specialist SD is a 14- pound, open-front stand ideal for bow hunting. —*DH*

Field-Judging Bucks

Become a master at gauging a buck's age by its body.

Odds are whether you already manage for big deer on your own land or you occasionally hunt with friends or outfitters on their properties, you're going to have to properly determine whether a buck is a "shooter" or not this season. In many places, such a determination is still a simple matter of deciding if the antlers meet established minimums on the property you're hunting. One club I occasionally hunt requires a buck to meet two of three measurements; the three minimums being 14 inches wide, 13 inches tall, and 30 mm across the base of one antler as measured by a micrometer. On my own property, it seems to be a sliding scale. I've been fortunate enough the past three years to take a pretty nice buck on opening day on the Virginia farm I hunt with family and a few close friends, and it seems no matter how big he is, it's never enough! But that's a topic for another column.

More and more, particularly when hunting with an outfitter, the requirement doesn't rest on antler size alone but on the age of the deer. Even if a buck has an 18-inch spread and sports 10 long points, few hunters in the know want to kill him if he's only two years old. After all, that buck still has a lot of growing to do, and no serious deer manager wants to see that potential eliminated from their land.

"The real trophy to me is taking an old buck, because he is going to be much harder to kill," Brian Murphy, executive director of the Quality Deer Management Association (QDMA), once told me. Indeed, aging a buck was never an issue just a few short years ago as long as the deer was big enough, but now, the more I travel, I almost regularly hear guys note they killed a nice three-year-old or a big four-year-old with the antler points and size almost secondary (though Boone & Crockett score is still always important, too!)

The QDMA (qdma.org) has a number of great resources available through its online store to help hunters and land managers better understand their local herd and how to properly grow it—and hunt it. The following is what to look for in various age classes of bucks to determine if it meets the minimums of wherever you may be hunting.

> More and more, particularly when hunting with an outfitter, the requirement doesn't rest on antler size alone but on the age of the deer.

1½-YEAR-OLD

This buck, with a narrow, pointed face, will look like a doe with antlers. His neck is also going to be slender, as are his legs, which will appear longish compared to the body—still almost as gangly-looking as they are when they're fawns. Don't think because it is a button or spike that it is a 1½-year-old, while a forky or other small-racked deer is at least a year older. Bucks in this age class can still sprout multiple tines; more antlers mean this guy has the potential to be a real bruiser if allowed to grow older. Regardless, the main beams will be narrow at the bases, and the overall rack will be thin. The tarsal glands at this age are small and light in coloration.

1½-YEAR-OLD

2½-YEAR-OLD

3½-YEAR-OLD

4½-YEAR-OLD

5½-YEAR-OLD

Notice the body progression in the photo sequence of this captive deer. Antlers can't always be trusted, as evidenced by the 4½-year-old's smaller, drought-depleted rack. Telltale signs on a deer's body, however, don't lie and are the best indications of how old a buck is. Photo Credits: George Barnett

2½-YEAR-OLD

Even with today's management mentality being drilled into us, statistically, few bucks ever live past this age class, accounting for the majority of racked bucks taken across the United States. The main reason is because the racks are filling out to eight and 10 points at this stage, and for hunters simply looking at points, it will be enough to yield the trophy they are seeking. But according to research, these bucks are really just beginning to develop. Their bodies are filling out more, but their backs and stomachs will still be flat and taut—the best way to tell if a broadside buck is still too young to shoot in most places today. The rump is also still squared, not rounded like an older buck, while the face still has a pointy look to it.

3½-YEAR-OLD

At this age, a buck's neck begins to thicken and his chest deepens, creating a more pronounced brisket that will curve up from its front legs. In fact, during the rut, the neck will actually be wider than the face for the first time. The nose on a 3½-year-old will also start to broaden, giving the buck the first glimmer of the stunted nose appearance an older trophy will have. The legs are also more in proportion with the rest of the body. The back and stomach are still pretty flat, though a slight curve is now apparent in the gut. The rump is beginning to look more rounded. The tarsal glands are getting darker, too, particularly during the rut. Antlers at this stage are getting impressive, often extending beyond the ears. Many hunters won't pass this buck up, though in reality, if he is somewhere you can keep hunting him, he still has a lot of growth to achieve given the chance.

4½-YEAR-OLD

Bucks are entering true trophy stage at this point, with a neck that is thicker than the head during the rut and ripples of muscle visible in their large but still trim body. Think of these bucks as athletes in their 20s. Most are in their physical—not necessarily antler—prime right now. The rump is completely rounded, tarsals are dark, and the legs are completely in proportion to their bodies and may in fact even appear a bit squat because their bodies have become so big. Not many hunters will pass up the better specimens in this age class. Racks are wide, tines are long, and the mass should make it so this buck is recognized as a shooter, not a borderline buck.

5½-YEAR-OLD

QDMA says at this age and beyond it becomes almost impossible for anybody but a biologist or studied hunter inspecting a dead buck's teeth to determine the buck's age on the hoof. Whether this buck is boasting ridiculous trophy antlers or landed in the shallow end of the gene pool and is still not making hunters gasp, it's time to pull this buck's card. Antlers at this age have reached virtually all of their potential. Physically, the buck's back and stomach are starting to sag from the increased weight gain we all seem to suffer as we get older. In fact, like an aging human, the skin will even begin to appear loose around the face. During the rut, the neck will swell so much and appear so muscular that his short, blunt face will look almost small. The deer will even develop a knock-kneed walk. Eyes are becoming squinty and tarsals are super dark. At this stage, a once-typical rack begins to take on nontypical features, such as sticker points and drop tines, which is why killing a 200-plus point typical is such a rarity. We can all only hope to meet up with a few 5½-year-old bucks in our lifetime, but if we pay attention to the age of the bucks we shoot and manage appropriately when possible, this will become more of a reality for more deer hunters. ⓗ

Rattle Trap

Take the hunt to a bruiser this fall and rattle him into range.

The more I deer hunt, the less I'm content to simply walk to my stand and passively sit and wait for a whitetail to amble by. Like the excitement I experience calling in turkeys, waterfowl, and, more recently, predators, I want to make something happen when I'm deer hunting. It's always great when the opportunity to shoot a big buck presents itself. It's even more rewarding when a call or stalk or other tactic I've tried actually brought that deer in close or put me in better position for the shot. Along those lines, rattling up whitetails has to be one of the best tactics I've ever tried, bringing in roughly 50 percent of the bucks I've shot in the last 10 years and accounting for the biggest ones I've killed. While some hunters will argue it's a tactic best suited for locales like Texas (where the technique began) where buck to doe ratios are near one to one or the Midwest where large open fields border smaller wood lots, if timed and done right rattling can produce in more wooded areas where does outnumber the boys. If you're not working it into your deer hunting mix, you need to reconsider. Done properly, it will forever change the way you hunt.

TIME IT RIGHT

When you rattle can be as important as how you rattle. Noted whitetail biologist Mickey Hellickson confirmed in a Texas study that the best

Be sure to incorporate rattling into your hunting setups. If done properly, it will forever change the way you hunt whitetails.

time to rattle is really a choice between quality and quantity. Mature bucks respond best during the pre-rut and even post-rut; most practiced hunters will say the seeking phase of the pre-rut, when bucks are most crazed with pent-up testosterone and still not overly pressured by hunters, is the time to work the antlers. However, according to Hellickson's research, the peak of the rut brought the most bucks running in. Despite a threefold increase in responses to rattling during the rut, a larger percentage of the bucks that came in were younger, immature deer. One theory is that the dominant bucks are already with does breeding, while the outliers are still seeking ready companions and are quick to check out sparring action since they're not locked down with a female. I've rattled up as many as 10 deer in a day, with the most positive responses coming in the last week of October through the second week of November. Hunter's Specialties Pro-Staffer Rick White says during the pre-rut he doesn't walk into the woods without a rattle bag.

MASTER THE PROCESS

One of the most important considerations before rattling is the same as choosing a stand location, and that is being concerned about the wind. A buck will almost always approach rattling from downwind, so choosing your location and controlling your scent is critical.

Setting up in a spot where a buck can't circle downwind is virtually impossible at times, but when you can, put a wide stream or creek or a steep bluff on your downwind side to eliminate a deer's approach from that direction. I simply prefer to set up off a young clearcut or field with the wind actually blowing into the open. That way, approaching bucks must expose themselves first. This is particularly good during gun season, when I can almost always get a shot at a bruiser before he gets close enough to cut my scent.

If it's still early in the pre-rut, start out softly tickling the antlers. Bucks may not yet be fighting hard, so soft rattling is often best and can bring bucks to your setup out of curiosity. As rutting action picks up, get more aggressive. Many hunters vary their routines (White doesn't even follow one, rattling softly at one time and hard another to see what works on a given day), but it's a good idea to begin aggressive rattling with a soft tickling of the antlers.

"Bucks don't typically start out with a loud clash, nor should you," says *Bloodline* host Alex Rutledge. Rattle soft at first, building up like two bucks are getting angrier and more intense. Rutledge and I both like to mix soft grunts with the rattling to increase realism as bucks, like humans lifting something heavy or struggling, will tend to grunt and groan during a battle. Rutledge even starts his rattling out with a buck growl, or roar, which he has heard bucks do as a challenge before fighting.

Rattle for two to three minutes and then wait 15 to 20 minutes before rattling again. Be sure to remain alert. It's not unusual for bucks to come running right in. Set up where you can see a long way and where you are

Rattling works equally well from a treestand or the ground. Play the wind properly, because bucks certainly will.

concealed—either high in a tree, in a blind, or behind a large tree or deadfall—to hide your movement while rattling, as any motion will easily be picked up.

For added realism, rake leaves and limbs, thrashing them with the antlers or your hands or feet if using a rattle bag. If hunting from a treestand, Rutledge will fill a sock with plastic bags and crunch it together to sound like deer's hooves crunching leaves. He also always uses a decoy if the rut is on.

"This gives the buck something visual to focus on as he approaches and simply adds to the realism of your setup," says Rutledge.

GO MOBILE

Many hunters rattle from the stand they plan to hunt all morning or evening, which works just fine. But rattling works great for the roving hunter, too. Seek out areas with lots of scrapes and rubs, which will reveal either an aggressive deer or a lot of deer in the area, both of which play into the hunter's hands. Identify bedding areas and set up 100 yards downwind, being sure to set where there is some concealment. You can catch bucks slipping from bedding cover or, if set up on a field or recent clearcut with the wind to your back, catch them as they enter the open. Follow the same tactics as the stand-bound hunter, and if nothing comes in, wait 30 minutes from the last rattle before moving 300 to 400 yards to a new spot and rattling again. This tactic can be the salvation for a hunter who finds it impossible to sit still for more than a couple of hours but who doesn't hunt terrain that lends itself to stalking. ⊞

Mastering Attractant Scents

Scents that appeal to a whitetail's need to feed, instead of an urge to breed, can be an important component to any hunt-day strategy.

A lot is written about scents for deer hunting. There are scents that trigger a buck's urge to breed by smelling like a doe in estrous or ones that fuel his desire to protect his domain by smelling like a challenging buck. There are scents designed to mask the odor of a human by covering it or molecularly bonding with it so a deer can't detect it. They are all designed with the hope of bringing in deer and keeping them calm once they are there.

But one important scent component is missing from the equation, particularly as we focus on the rut and spend more time contemplating a big buck's need to breed rather than feed at this time of year. That component is attractant scents —ones that smell like food and can be used to draw deer in and put them at ease, keeping them hanging out in an area longer until they provide the perfect shot opportunity. Even when smaller bucks, does and yearlings are what arrive, they can serve as live decoys, attracting a bigger buck on to the scene the longer they remain in the area.

Attractant scents are an important consideration in areas where baiting is permitted, as they can enhance the natural

Even during the rut, not all scents should focus around sex. Does still want to eat, even though bucks may not. Draw the females into your area with food scents, and bucks will likely follow.

attraction of foods, whether planted or dispersed from a feeder, by creating more scent to drift out on thermals and breezes and bring in deer from farther away. However, their true benefit can be realized by many hunters who live in areas where baiting is illegal.

Depending on how a state's laws are written, bait is most often defined as it is in Virginia's code, as "any food, grain or other consumable substance that could serve as a lure or attractant," food plots and other naturally grown crops notwithstanding, of course. That means attractant scents are a go in such areas and can help draw deer into a spot that is nutritionally void or enhance the already magnetizing effect a food plot has on deer.

BENEFITS

While enhancing food sources with additional scent certainly is a good use for these products, without a doubt the best benefits will be experienced by sportsmen who live or hunt in states where baiting is illegal.

In talking about Code Blue's Urge, a product that arouses a deer's sense of smell and taste as well as increases its appetite, company spokesman Mike Mattly notes how when it first came out, it was only available in powder form.

"Urge was originally made as a powder only, which many states consider bait," says Mattly. "If a deer can see it and put it in its mouth and eat it, then it's a bait." The company, in recognizing the extended benefits such an attractant could have in places where baiting isn't permitted, then came up with a liquid version.

"In liquid form, it can be used and applied the same way a hunter would use deer urine," says Mattly. "All it is is a scent, which makes it safe to use in areas where baiting is illegal."

What's even better is the convenience with which such sprays are applied. For the hunter who doesn't want to lug bags of corn to his lease (where baiting is allowed) or spend time working and growing food plots, attractant scents can provide another avenue for bringing in deer. Urge, or similar products such as Wildgame Innovation's Cornfused or even Primos' spray-on Swamp Donkey, can be toted in small, easily packable spray bottles and misted on existing plants near a stand. This is particularly helpful in enhancing remote stand locations. Some brands, such as Wildgame's Corn In Heat and Acorn In Heat, also combine food scents with urine scents to appeal to the whitetails' needs on a combination of levels—a particular bonus during the rut.

Another key benefit Mattly points out is how these attractants will stop a deer in its tracks, helping to ensure a stationary, broadside target.

"A lot of hunters will bleat at a jogging buck to get him to stop before shooting, but if you can get him to stop without having to give your location away with sound, it's a much better option," Mattly says.

BEST USE TRICKS

To get the most out of attractant sprays, try the following:

- Spray attractants on the leaves of plants where deer are likely to eat anyway when possible. Mulberry, laurel, honeysuckle and soft mast such as grapes are all good options.

The sprays will greatly enhance the attractiveness of these areas. Gels can be applied directly to the bark of trees with good success.

- In the absence of natural food sources, be sure to still spray food scents on leaves and limbs at least four to five feet off the ground in order to catch thermals and breezes and increase the product's effectiveness. Don't waste its benefits by simply spraying it on the ground.

- Food-based scents can be a better option than urine-based ones early in the season before rut activity since bucks, as well as does, are still interested in feeding.

- During the rut, however, don't ignore food-based attractants. Wildgame Innovation's Major Person says food is in less supply as autumn wears on and the weather turns cold, so does will be actively seeking it out. The more does in an area, the more bucks will show up as well.

- When hunting adjacent to a bedding area or active deer trails, apply scents so that their odor will drift downwind into the areas where deer will be bedded or on the move.

- When applying scents around your stand, be sure to spray them in two to three spots along open shooting lanes since deer will stop to check them out as they pass. Avoid spraying them where you can't get a shot.

- Feel free to experiment, but most hunters will find that attractant scents that smell like foods natural to their area will often perform better than scents that are unfamiliar to the local herd. For example, when hunting an oak flat, use an acorn-scented spray.

- Don't forget, attractant scents can pull double duty as good cover scents and often smell a lot better than fox urine or other products. ⬩

Prepare Your Deer Woods Now

There is much to do to get your land ready for the season.

The mercury is soaring, but cooler deer hunting weather will be here in no time, which means now is when you need to get your land in order. Planting fall food plots is a start, but properly getting your land ready for the coming season goes well beyond seed in the ground. From identifying natural food sources and bedding areas to repositioning stands and clearing lanes, there is plenty you can do in the heat of late summer that will pay big dividends down the road.

IDENTIFY NEW BEDDING COVER

The forest is a dynamic place, changing from year to year. Recently cut areas with abundant sunlight grow thick, while established woodlands or pine plantations open up as the perpetual shade suppresses the understory. Areas where deer bedded one year may not hold them the next. It's critical to identify these spots and understand their proximity to current food sources. Even if you've hunted a property for years, it pays to slip some boots on, spray down with insect repellant, and take a hike through the key areas you'll be hunting this fall.

On a fairly current aerial photo, mark areas where there are newly fallen trees, knocked down by storms and high summer winds, the tops of which will provide excellent bedding cover for big whitetails in otherwise open areas. Deer love to lie in these tops because they can remain hidden while watching for danger to approach from a distance.

Cutover areas that have enjoyed two to four years of growth will hold tons of deer in the fall. They will hold

Rechecking all your stands before the season starts is a far better idea than during the predawn stillness of opening morning.

deer afterwards as well, but in that two- to four-year range the height of the growth is perfect for hunter and deer alike. The weeds and brush are tall enough to make deer feel secure when bedding and moving through it, yet hunters in elevated stands along the edges can still see—and shoot—deer as they move through the cover. Bucks will also work these edges during the rut, trying to intercept the scent of a receptive doe. Find a young cutover bordering ag fields or a food plot and you've found your money spot.

Likewise, stands of pines or young trees that are maturing and that once held bedded deer may have opened up so much that deer no longer use them. It can be pointless to keep a once productive stand in these areas when moving it near a new bedding area might serve you better.

INSPECT THE MAST

During your walk, keep an eye out for natural foods as well. One of the biggest factors that can determine whether deer will be actively feeding in open fields and plots early in the season, or remain hidden in the woods, is the state of the mast crop—particularly acorns. Oaks don't always produce. In fact, acorn production can be quite variable depending on a long list of factors. Even years when a number of trees seem to produce, not all of them will.

According to Whitetail Stewards Inc.'s Matt Tarr, the best time to conduct an acorn survey is between the second and last week of August. At that time, acorns have developed enough to be visible from the ground, while acorn predators, such as squirrels, will not have eaten too much of the crop. Using binoculars, inspect the tops of oaks for limbs laden with the sweet-tasting nuts. White oaks are preferred to red oaks, but both provide important nutrition. If oaks are abundant,

plan on focusing early-season hunts in the woods, as big bucks prefer the safety of cover to feeding in the open. Likewise, if only a few scattered trees are thick with acorns, these trees will be some of the most serious deer magnets come this fall.

CLEAR A PATH

Accessing a stand during hunting season without alerting the local deer population is critical. Many hunters give ample thought to which stand to hunt depending on wind direction but never give a second thought to if the way they're walking into that stand will blow their scent through the area they plan to hunt. Choose a way to access each stand consistent with the wind conditions in which you will be hunting it and then clear a path through the woods with a hard metal rake. The key now is to remove existing leaf litter and, more importantly, underlying sticks and branches that can crack and pop beneath the weight of a boot. When new leaves begin falling in autumn, hit the trail with a rake again if at all possible without disturbing a hunting area.

Don't forget to trim overhanging limbs away from your path to reduce the number of places you have to touch on the way into a stand. This will limit the amount of human scent you potentially trail through the woods on the way in. With a clear, downwind path to access your stand, you can actually hang stands tighter to potential big buck bedding areas, improving your odds of remaining undetected.

FIND THE OTHER FOODS

Other top natural foods include muscadines, persimmons, dogwoods, honeysuckle, clover, berries, and old fruit trees. Deer also browse fresh green shoots of almost any type, so areas that have been burned over can provide a smorgasbord. Planted fields of soybean, alfalfa, corn, and wheat will draw deer better than most natural foods, but it's just as important to note what has been planted on adjoining properties as well as your own, as these can draw deer away from your property.

CREATE BUCK STRUCTURE

Want to create a deer magnet in the middle of an otherwise unbroken forest? Get together with a few friends one weekend, grab your chainsaws, and go in and clear out an open area in the middle of the woods. It doesn't have to be big—40 to 60 yards wide and maybe a little longer. By doing this, you will not only create an immediate bedding area with the felled trees, but whitetails will feed on the now accessible leaves. Sunlight will also reach the ground in this spot, spawning new growth each summer and providing natural browse in a mature stand of timber otherwise devoid of it. Naturally, if you don't own the land, be sure you get the landowner's permission because those trees could equal money to them.

This new cover provides a great spot for bucks to lie during the rut and keep tabs on does as they pass through the area. Hang a stand nearby, and you'll be set come this November.

CHECK, HANG STANDS

Now is the time to rethink where you want to hang stands. Take in mind prevailing winds in each feeding and bedding area as well as the travel of the sun from east to west to ensure you won't be staring into the sun at the time of day you expect to be hunting the stand most often. Hang the stand where other limbs will provide some natural cover behind you, but don't forget to clear at least four to five shooting lanes in every direction around the stand.

For stands that were left hanging throughout the offseason, check straps for wear and bolts and steps for rust and tightness. Replace or fix anything that looks worn or loose so that the stand is safe for use. Fix squeaking ladders, platforms, and seats as nothing can ruin a hunt quicker than popping metal as you shift to take aim. ⓗ

Midwest Whitetails On Your Own

Think a whitetail hunt requires expensive access? Think again.

H e approached from atop a flat over-looking a cedar-choked drainage where I had hung my stand. All I could see of him through the chest-deep CRP was the top of his back and the shape of his antlers. I didn't even try to count tines—one glance at the buck's frame was all the confirmation I needed. If given a chance, I would shoot this deer.

While I had arrived in Kansas just two days prior to my encounter, the hunt began months in advance. As a resident of Colorado, I'm almost ashamed to admit that I had never traveled to the well-known whitetail honey hole that exists right next door. I guess I dragged my feet a bit because I didn't have any contacts in Kansas and wasn't quite sure where to go. Then last year, I finally asked myself, what are you waiting for?

In my younger days, I spent some of my fondest bow-hunting memories chasing whitetails with a good friend named Jamie Beauxis. We were in our early twenties at the time, and neither of us had a proverbial pot-to-piss-in, but that never stopped us. Nebraska, Missouri, and Iowa (when we could draw a tag) were some of our favorite Midwestern haunts. We would often hit the road with scarcely enough cash to cover our gasoline, and we spent many a cold November night sleeping in the cab of our pickup trucks. We scouted on-the-fly as we stopped to visit small public hunting lands we had located on our maps. Even if one of us had owned a computer at the time, resources like Google Earth weren't available back then. The only way to get familiar with an area was to lay

eyes on it and burn boot leather. These were the humblest of hunting adventures to say the least, but our passion for bowhunting whitetails was overpowering, and we were blind to any adversity.

I learned more about bowhunting whitetails on those outings than I have in all the years since. Jamie and I managed a pretty decent success ratio during those years, and although we weren't taking what most would consider trophy deer, we savored each as though it were Boone and Crockett caliber. What I enjoyed most about those hunts, however, was that there was no one to blame and no one to thank. The man in the mirror was solely responsible for any success, or lack thereof, and that, my friends, can be a very satisfying feeling.

When the time came to apply for the Kansas draw, I decided to go back to my roots. With all of the resources available today, there's really no reason a motivated bowhunter can't locate a few reasonably good pieces of public hunting ground.

My first step in this process was to visit the Kansas Department of Wildlife, Parks and Tourism website (kdwpt.state.ks.us) to do a little research. It didn't take long to learn that Kansas offers plenty of public hunting opportunity. Between public wildlife areas and their Walk-In Hunting Access program (WIHA), Kansas provides public access to more than one million acres of hunting land.

The next step was to narrow down a general area. I did this by breaking out the latest version of the Pope & Young record book. The 17th Edition, released in 2011, comes with a disc that allows you to sort every entry by county, state, and date. This makes gauging what counties currently offer bowhunters the greatest odds of success on Pope & Young-class animals. Once I had decided on a county, I returned to the KDWPT website to find information on which game management unit I would need to apply for and to reference maps of public hunting areas on the Kansas Hunting Atlas. I then printed the maps and used Google Earth to further investigate each parcel of public hunting land, searching the detailed aerial images and geographic contours to identify desirable cover and topography. By the time I was done, I had a handful of public hunting areas I knew I wanted to check out.

Next, I contacted the terrestrial biologist responsible for the public areas I was interested in. This is where you might want to pay attention. After informing the biologist of my intentions, I immediately asked about the parcel that looked most appealing on Google Earth. I was surprised when he told me that he would not recommend the parcel to a bowhunter. I asked why, and he responded, "That's overgrown with cedars and CRP." Cedars and CRP, I thought to myself! What the heck is the problem again?

I'm still not sure what led him to think that little piece of land wouldn't be productive. Perhaps he hunted it himself from time-to-time and was trying to protect it. Or maybe, since there were few trees there capable of holding a treestand, he thought it might make bowhunting difficult. The point is, when I finally arrived at the property, I took one look and knew that guy didn't know what on earth he was talking about. When conducting this kind of research, contact whoever you can to gather information on hunting ground, but take what they tell you with a grain of salt. And by all means, trust your instincts. If your gut tells you to dig a little deeper, then keep digging.

Like I said, when I arrived in Kansas, all it took was a quick look over the parcel in question to know I was in a great spot. And best of all, there were no signs of other bowhunters!

I spent my first day doing as much low-impact scouting as possible. I chose a couple of likely stand locations and decided to set up the next morning. However, dawn the following day brought torrential rains, so I spent a second day scouting other locations. On day three, I finally made my way into position, set up my stand, and climbed in. I was scarcely there more than a few minutes when I spotted deer movement. A yearling buck walked below my stand, made a scrape, and then continued into the cedars to bed. An hour later, I spotted the buck that began this story.

After crossing the CRP flat, the buck disappeared behind some cedars less than 50 yards from my stand. He soon reappeared, following the same path along the drainage that the younger buck had followed. At 30 yards he turned and approached my stand head-on. Then suddenly, at less than 15 yards, the wind swirled. As he began testing the air, I could tell this might not go as I had hoped. He stood for close to a minute before deciding that something was just not right. As he swapped ends, I drew my bow and grunted him to a stop. When he looked over his shoulder, I released the string.

Moments later, I recovered my first buck from the Sunflower State. I must say, in hindsight, I was a little disappointed to go all that way and have my hunt end so early. I do wonder what else I might have seen had I been more patient. However, as was the case during the humble public land whitetail adventures I experienced in my younger years, I was more than satisfied with the results of the hard work I put into this hunt. When all was said and done, I looked in the mirror, gave myself a pat on the back, then pointed my truck west and headed home. Ⓗ

Last Shot Bucks

The final days of deer season are upon you. Make them count.

I'm not going to lie: I'm not crazy about hunting deer during the late season. The weather is colder, the rut is over, and fewer deer are on the move. Hunter pressure has been brutal. As a result, two hours on a stand can feel like an entire day. Hunters who have been going at it hard are as worn-out as the bucks they're hunting. But for those who remain focused, this is a great time of the season to topple truly big deer.

"The post-estrous period can actually be better than the seeking phase of the rut. You won't see as many deer, but you will see some monsters," says big buck slayer and outdoor TV legend Mark Drury. "You might sit for days without seeing many deer and then the biggest deer you've ever seen will walk right in."

The name of the game at this time of year is to find the food. Bucks are worn slap out after chasing every hot doe whose path they cross, and with brutal cold descending upon major swaths of the whitetail's range, food is essential to restore energy and survive the winter. If you're a member of the unfortunate crowd still looking to fill a buck tag with a real season-making bruiser, your first job is to find the food—your second is to find the buck visiting it.

FOOD IS YOUR FOCUS

Like a buck, you need to identify what in your hunt area is going to provide the most nutritious food for the local herd—possibly a challenge this winter after the brutal drought experienced throughout many areas this past summer. The first choice will be agricultural fields—preferably ones that were planted with corn, soybeans, alfalfa, or the like. Most will be cut by now, but deer will hit them looking for remnants scattered on the ground. In some areas where corn has been left standing for wildlife, pay particular attention, as standing corn not only provides food but also cover, so deer can feed and bed in one spot, something a wary buck will prefer given the likely hunting pressure he has already experienced.

"When it is cold, we hunt over grains," says Drury. "When it is warm, we go to the greens." The latter meaning planted food plots or perhaps fields where soybeans are still uncut as deer don't require the excessive protein found

Adam Hays says hunters need to take the time to scout during the season in order to pattern big bucks. Hays killed this 182-inch late-season giant on one of those scouting trips.

in grains if it is not as cold. The good thing about greens, too, is it digests more quickly in a deer, so they get on their feet more often to feed. If you have food plots planted in leafy, frost-sweetening brassicas, such as turnips or kale, you have the second most likely spot whitetails will head to feed. Leave one or two of these hot spots alone. Let deer get comfortable going and coming into them for a week or two if you can spare the time, and then hit them only when the time is right. (More on that in a minute.)

Lastly, alternate food sources now will be old oak stands where acorns fell earlier in the season. Like in the crop fields, deer will return, digging among the leaves for remnants. Hawthorn, soft mast (such as dogwoods), and wild berries will all be a draw as will old apples, pears, and persimmons. Beechnuts will also attract deer when other high-protein mast is scarce. Find these spots

SNORT-WHEEZE MAGIC

Like Michael Waddell, who claims the snort-wheeze is "the killingest call" ever, big buck hunter Adam Hays has also enjoyed a fair amount of excellent success using the call, even in the late season, after observing large bucks acting aggressively toward others. In fact, the late-season giant he killed a couple years ago was one that he actually snort-wheezed in from an observation stand. Hays, a dedicated bowhunter, always carries his bow along even on in-season scouting missions since, as in this case, he never knows when a big boy will show up. "I saw how aggressive he was behaving and decided to give a snort-wheeze a try," Hays says. The buck came right in.

I used the same call last year to kill my buck on the opening day of firearms season, as shooting time was winding down. With low light a factor and the deer too far to see my crosshairs on its dark hide, I snort-wheezed in conjunction with a decoy and the buck came stomping right in to 60 yards. The closer range made it easier to see where my reticle was resting on the animal, and I crushed him with my Winchester SXP slug gun. *–D.H.*

and watch them. Now you have to figure out which ones are receiving antlered visitors at a time you can hunt them.

SCOUT FIRST

Ohio hunter and *Intrepid Outdoors* co-host Adam Hays is an elite big buck hunter. He is one of only two hunters with as many as three 200-plus-inch deer to his credit, and he has a good number of bucks that have tapped out at more than 170 and even 180 inches. One of his nicest giants was a 182-inch 10-point that he scored late in the season, a time of year he admits he isn't as gung-ho about hunting, either.

"I really prefer early season to any other time of the year, because a buck's feeding pattern makes him more predictable and hunter pressure isn't a huge factor yet," says Hays. "After that, the post-rut is good because they are returning to feeding patterns. Even though they have been pressured, if you can locate a good buck and pattern him, you can kill him." For that reason, even as the season rages on, Hays takes time to scout from a distance in order to get as much intel on when and how and in what conditions a buck visits a food source before actually hunting the buck. For that reason, he focuses most of his late season efforts on deer hitting larger food plots and fields, since he can set up at a distance and observe, for days if necessary, before actually hunting the buck. It's a tip he learned after reading an article about deer hunting great Myles Keller.

"It's what Myles Keller called hunting from the outside in," says Hays. "Before going into an area, I will sit an observation stand as far from the area I think the deer is feeding in as I can get." Hays will then watch how a deer enters an area, as well as how it leaves it, noting the moon phase, wind direction, temperature, and any other key observation that will help him set up properly.

"That way when it's time to hunt the buck, I'll know the exact wind to hunt it in and the exact tree to set my stand on," he says. When the conditions match those he observed the deer in, he moves in for the kill, quickly setting up his climbing sticks (four sections) and hang-on immediately before he hunts the spot. The effort pays off. Hays has killed the eight biggest bucks of his life (both early and late season) the first evening he sat a stand.

"Don't ever hunt an area until it's right," he says. "It only takes one mistake to blow a big deer out of an area, especially late in the season." Ⓗ

Navigating The October Lull

Can anyone prove (or disprove) the mysterious October vanishing act known as "the lull"?

Do you believe in the October lull? It's a question every dedicated whitetail hunter has had to tackle at some point. Most of the time it's on the fifth straight all-day sit without even a hint or a sniff of that monster buck you've been seeing on the food plot all fall (this has happened to me twice in the last three years). He's gone, the trail cameras are quiet, and no matter how many times you move your stand or adjust your setup, he's not coming out to play. You might as well cash it in and wait for his rut-inspired reappearance.

It's not as if this is some mythical happening. We know the general parameters in which the lull occurs, but even so, there's no magical formula or code that will crack this case. I put down the treasure map long ago; this "X" is a moving target. And without hunting your property (which I'm completely willing to do...I'm a dedicated journalist), I can't give too much advice on any particular conundrum.

In general, though, this is a question of cause and effect. We're all aware that there is a period of time in mid

to late October in which big bucks become less visible. Some hunters just simply take a break during this time of year, leaving the woods unpressured, while others have consistent success. Whether it's luck or strategy, if you want to navigate the October lull with success, you must first determine how much of the conventional "wisdom" about deer movement is backed up by tangible evidence.

It's time to stop attaching our own rationale to unexplainable big buck behavior and look to some data for answers.

THE THEORIES

There are several factors contained in theories explaining this decline in buck sightings. These are generally the same reasons why whitetails alter their movements or patterns any other time of year: food, breeding cycles, hunter pressure, and herd dynamics. It just so happens that in October all or most of these variables begin to change at once.

In the early season and during heavy scouting in July and August, whitetails can be rather predictable. Biologists know that deer are crepuscular, meaning that they move and feed primarily at low light (dawn and dusk).

They travel from bedding areas to meal spots on a schedule, with bucks convening in bachelor groups. Deer are consistently visible (and huntable) near open food sources during this period.

As the season progresses toward October, primary food sources (row crops like soybeans) are no longer a lush, replenished snack for bucks. Much has been harvested, and other sources are yellow and dry. Acorns are starting to fall, and other mast crops are dropping in the timber. As food sources change, so do deer patterns. Bucks are moving into fall ranges and preparing for the rut.

Archery seasons are also in full swing in October, and hunters are beginning to pour into the woods. Many believe this uptick in human activity is another reason for the lull. Bucks become nocturnal, moving at night to avoid the ire of hunters and other increasing pressures. But are all of these variables really contributing to the lull? Or are we just doing our best to categorize the symptoms of a problem we can't explain?

RIGHT MOVES

The lull is based on buck movement, or lack thereof, so tracking every step a buck takes from the beginning to the end of hunting season is logically the best way to tackle this problem.

That's what researchers around the country have begun to do over the past few years with varying levels of success.

Andy Olson conducted one such study in 2012 as a part of his thesis for his master's degree at the University of Georgia's Warnell School of Forestry and Natural Resources. Olson, who studied under the direction of renowned biologist Dr. Karl V. Miller, used GPS collar technology to study spatial and movement ecology of big bucks in northern Pennsylvania. The study's objectives were to "document and compare fine-scale temporal movements during breeding and hunting seasons."

Olson and his colleagues were able to collect significant data from three different bucks from January to December. Other studied deer were killed by hunters, lost, or simply had an interruption in data collection.

The GPS collars provided data points every hour until October 1st, when they began to provide movement updates every 15 minutes. Olson deemed breeding activity to begin in October, determining from previous data that this month can be categorized as the pre-rut, November the rut, and December the post-rut. My first question was simple: Inside the three months of your designated "breeding" phase was there any lull in buck movement?

"No, not at all," Olson said. "My data does not support any lull theories. There was no significant lower movement during the month of October for any of the deer we studied."

How would he describe the tracking data?

"The movement for the three bucks mirrored a simple bell curve," he said. "It began to pick up in early October and continued to rise through November and dropped back off to similar levels through the post rut in December."

Olson went on to explain that he saw no real uptick in nighttime movements until deer began chasing and searching for a breeding partner in November, and even then, the bucks' movements increased across the board.

"The only significant change was daytime buck activity increasing four to eight times during the peak rut," he said.

Nothing in the study lent credence to assertions that bucks go nocturnal during October or adjust their home ranges due to increased hunting pressure.

"We had hunters that encountered these bucks during the season, and not one buck changed his home range," he said. "If a buck detects you, he's not going to leave or stop moving, he's going to travel differently within his area."

From the outside looking in, it seems that Olson's study backs up most of the conventional wisdom about big buck movement (the rut increase, home range identification, and others) except the October lull.

"My biggest take away was that bucks don't disappear or go silent," he said. "If you're not seeing him, don't give up. If he's alive, that trophy is still around and on the move ...very close." Ⓗ

Still-Hunting Bucks

Taking a trophy whitetail while slipping through the woods is one of the most rewarding feats in hunting.

A long sit the day prior revealed bucks were chasing heavily, but in the randomness of the rut, none ambled under my stand. That night a front turned the south wind inside out and hauled with it a November rain that rendered potato chip leaves into pool table felt. So the next morning I audibled to a new attack. I set out into the wind, sloth-like, pausing every few feet to examine new slices of woods unveiled by each methodic step.

I actually smelled his tarsals before I saw him. The buck cruised across me, curious-eyed, 30 yards away. I spied 5 points, a matching side, and decent width. I nudged the safety off my .308 and found the buck's chest in my scope as he cleared an oak.

With my hand on the buck's still-warm chest, I had a thought: Hunting whitetails from treestands is mighty effective, but it's surely not as fun.

THE STILL-HUNTING TECHNIQUE

Still-hunting, or slip-hunting as some call it, is the technique of sneaking through the woods on foot and using all of your senses to get within range of an animal or to put yourself in a position to let it get within range of you.

The challenge is to see a deer before it sees you. This means you must move so slowly that your overall movement becomes as imperceptible to the fauna as a clock's hour hand is to you. It requires placing a foot ahead of the other as if it were in slow motion, then pausing for a minute before moving the next. It requires being aware of your silhouette at all times. It also requires a Zen-like attitude and flowing with the woods to use what it gives you to your advantage. Most of your time should be spent not moving your feet, but inspecting the woods ahead of you with your eyes. Your best tool is a binocular, and it should seldom leave your hand.

I hold my 10x32 binos in my right hand so I can cradle my rifle in my left arm with its butt under my armpit, barrel forward and down. Keeping my right elbow tucked to my side, I raise the glass to my eye with

Still hunting is challenging, yet rewarding. Still hunt during the rut or after a recent rain for best results.

minimal movement. If I could glue them to my face, I would. Vision at 10X allows me to pick apart subtle edges and colors among the vegetation that could be a part of an animal, and it allows me to see through the woods that otherwise distracts and hampers my normal vision. A binocular harness is handy. Leave the lens caps in the truck; if it's raining, cover the ocular lenses.

When you lower your binocular to take a small step, scan the woods with your eyes, looking for flickering light that betrays movement. I take a slow step, glass, scan, and repeat. Stalking in this fashion takes incredible mental discipline, and if you're doing it right, you'll notice how quickly you'll become tired and hungry. Take a break when you begin to get impatient—it will become obvious when you start making clumsy mistakes—as that's precisely the time you'll spook something. Take that break in a spot where you'll possibly see a buck.

If you can hear yourself walking, you're too loud. If deer routinely see you before you see them, you're going too fast and not glassing enough. When you get it right, you'll notice how many deer you see before they see you.

CONFLUENCE OF CONDITIONS

For best success still-hunting bucks, you'll need the rut, recent rain, and the wind in your favor.

The rut dulls a buck's danger impulse by a half-step. That second-long pause is often all a hunter needs when hunting with a rifle. (It's much more difficult with a bow, but it can be done.)

A whitetail uses its ears like radar beacons, so it's nearly impossible to stalk one when the forest is laden with dry leaves. So for all but the Natty Bumppos among us, still-hunt only among damp or otherwise quiet ground. And if the wind isn't right, don't bother still-hunting. You'll benefit from a steady breeze that pulls your scent away from whitetails ahead of you, and it also masks your sound. Move only when the wind blows, and if it shifts, turn into it. Take advantage of the opportunities the rut offers you to bag a Booner buck from a stalk.

CHALLENGES OF STALKING BUCKS

When a seasoned still-hunter gets the right conditions, killing a deer from the ground is easy; it's trophy hunting that's tough. Because the vast majority of deer in the field are not shooter-quality bucks, most deer encountered while stalking are passed by the trophy hunter. These deer often flow around the hunter as they continue foraging. Eventually, they'll cross the hunter's wind trail and spook, alerting other deer. So spooking deer while trophy hunting is a part of the game. But if you continue to slip within killing range of deer, it's only a matter of time until you get in range of a shooter who's thinking about his next date instead of his own safety.

JUDGING ON THE HOOF

When you see movement through the woods, immediately get your binocular on it to identify it as a deer and then move to its head to see if it's a buck. At close range—inside 50 yards—it's often best to lower the binocular and use your eyes to get a relative view of a buck's rack compared to its body. When a deer is moving in thick woods, you'll seldom have time to examine each tine. If you determine he's a shooter, get him in your crosshairs, click the safety off, and hammer him the very first opportunity you get.

GEAR MUST-HAVES

Fleece or wool is best for stalking. Pants and jackets that crinkle and swish are not worth having. Because I most often stalk on damp ground or in the rain and I frequently stop to sit, I prefer water-resistant, breathable pants that are quiet, like Core 4 Element's Highline pant. In a light rain I add a waterproof jacket and hat. (A hood restricts peripheral vision.) Wear thin gloves to camouflage the hand's constant movement while raising a binocular. Wear flexible, soft-soled boots that are waterproof—something like a Scent-Lok Silent Stalk Sneaker. This is no time for rubber boots. Don't worry about insulation—you'll be active. If you get serious about stalking, consider leather moccasins over Gore-Tex socks. Leave the backpack and all the other brush-snagging gadgets at home. If you must carry a bag, consider the Browning Billy 1000 Lumbar Pack. It's small and goes around your waist, limiting snags. Ⓗ

WHITETAIL AMMO:
Understanding The Difference

Why hunt with a deer-specific cartridge? The answer is easy.

A few years ago, someone decided that we needed to shoot premium bullets at every game animal we hunted. If it wasn't a Triple-Shock, AccuBond, Scirocco, or XP3, it wasn't worth loading into your magazine. The performance of most of these bullets is amazing, but some hunters decided they didn't need a bullet designed to penetrate a zebra lengthwise to kill a broadside white-tail at a distance of half of a football field. Other hunters found that premium bullets designed with terminal performance in mind didn't always produce good accuracy. The industry responded with loads designed and marketed specifically for whitetail hunting without expensive premium bullets. These "whitetail" loads use lead core ammunition at traditional velocities and are offered at prices lower than the premium loads. What was old is now new again.

So what do we want a whitetail bullet to do? Most whitetail hunters are looking for fairly rapid expansion that will induce massive trauma on the animal, followed by penetration that will result in at least some substantial part of the bullet transecting the body of the deer. These bullets tend to be "softer" than most premium designs and offer more expansion and less penetration, which is fine so long as you pick your shots

accordingly. Such bullets are relatively easy to manufacture and are, therefore, available at a lower price than premium designs that require more intricate procedures and pricier component materials.

Let's take a look at four of the most common whitetail-specific product lines on the market.

REMINGTON
WHITETAIL PRO CORE-LOKT

Remington never really left the party when it came to whitetail-specific ammunition. Its Core-Lokt bullet has been around for over 75 years and remains a standby for whitetail hunting. The bullet was considered a groundbreaking premium design at its introduction since it mechanically controlled expansion and produced consistent mushrooms on game. Bullet technology has long surpassed the Core-Lokt when it comes to deep-penetrating and expanding

designs, but it is still the standard by which other "cup and core" whitetail bullets are judged.

The Core-Lokt not only is a solid performer, but also is available in factory ammunition for a wide variety of cartridges, including some unusual ones, such as the .300 Savage, .303 British, and .35 Remington. Though these cartridges don't get much, if any, love from the outdoor media these days, there are plenty of them in the hands of whitetail hunters across the nation, and they kill deer just as dead as they did before World War II. Core-Lokts aren't setting any records for ballistic coefficient, but that matters little to 90 percent of deer hunters. It's hard to beat this classic when it comes to putting deer in the freezer.

WINCHESTER
DEER SEASON XP

Winchester's deer-specific load is called the Deer Season XP, and it is probably the most explosive of the designs discussed here. Winchester's whitetail line differs from the other brands in that it utilizes a polymer-tipped bullet to facilitate expansion and provide a slightly higher ballistic coefficient. Bullets in this line are light-for-caliber and are loaded to fairly high

velocities. This load is designed to expand rather violently and create a massive wound channel, exactly what some whitetail hunters are looking for. I wouldn't expect many exit wounds when using these bullets, so if deep penetration is your thing, look elsewhere. Winchester's cartridge selection is fairly limited with loads available for eight common cartridges, including the .243, .270, and .300 WSM.

HORNADY
AMERICAN WHITETAIL

Hornady's whitetail line uses the company's long-proven InterLock bullet, which I've often heard described as a "poor man's premium" due to its excellent terminal performance and low price. The InterLock uses a tapered jacket and a locking ring to mechanically control the expansion of the bullet on game. The bullet acts a bit like a Nosler Partition: The front expands, and sometimes fragments,

while the shank stays intact and penetrates deeply. I have used handloaded InterLock bullets on countless deer, feral hogs, and a black bear and have never witnessed anything but great performance. Just last year I used a 162-grain InterLock at very close range on an Alabama whitetail buck, and despite an impact velocity of well over 3,000 fps, the bullet exited after dropping him where he stood. My own experience has taught me that InterLock bullets often produce exit wounds on broadside shots, a virtue I hold in high regard. Hornady's American Whitetail ammo is loaded in 10 common whitetail cartridges, including the .25-06, .30-30 WCF, and the 7mm Remington Magnum.

FEDERAL
PREMIUM FUSION

Federal was one of the pioneers in offering premium bullets made by nonaffiliated companies in its loaded ammunition line. This was a great thing for hunters who didn't handload, but it created a price and performance gap. Federal created the whitetail-focused Fusion line to fill this important niche.

While Hornady and Remington use similar mechanical means to control expansion and keep the bullet's lead core attached to the jacket, Federal uses a more modern molecular bonding method to "fuse" the elements. In theory, the jacket and core in a bonded bullet such as the Fusion cannot separate, which means the bullet will not "blow up" on the shoulder when shot at close range.

The Fusion is available in a broad variety of cartridges, from the .223 Remington to big-bore magnums, such as the .458 Lott, and even includes a deer-appropriate load for the often-underrated 7.62x39mm. The Fusion is a tough bullet I wouldn't hesitate to drive through the shoulder bones of a big buck at close range. Ⓗ

The following articles were previously published in *Petersen's Hunting*:

"Whiteout Whitetails," 2010 Hunting Annual; "A Kiwi Whitetail" and "Big Buck Lessons," April 2010; "Midwest Whitetails" and "Crushed Velvet," August 2010; "493 Dead Deer," October 2010; "Under Pressure: See More Deer Throughout the Season," April 2011; "How Much Does Size Matter," July 2011; "The Bucks of Summer, " September 2011; "The Ultimate Whitetail Decoy," "Ultimate Deer Surveillance," and Mastering Attractant Scents, " October 2011; "The Rut–Don't Screw it Up," November 2011; "Post-Rut in Kansas," December 2011-January 2012; "Backpack Your Buck," March 2012; "Under Pressure: Here's How to Use it—and Lose it—To Your Advantage," April-May 2012, "Early Season Deer Primer," June-July 2012; "Prepare Your Deer Woods Now," August 2012; "Field-Judging Bucks, " September 2012; 10 Ways to Score Big in the Pre-Rut," October 2012; "Seeing is Believing," "Tweak His Nose," Rattle Trap,"and Midwest Whitetails On Your Own," November 2012; "Tag Out Now!" and "Last Shot Bucks," December 2012-January 2013; The Top 7 Tractor Implements for the Food Plotter," April-May 2013; "Mule Deer vs Whitetails," October 2013; "A Really Special Deer Rifle" and "Western Paradise," November 2013; "Navigating the October Lull," October 2013; "Back 2 Basics: 10 Classic Rut Strategies That Still Work," November 2015; "Still-Hunting Bucks" and "Understanding Whitetail Ammo," December 2015-January 2016